Catherine Gourlat

Weaving in Style

Photographs by Elizabeth Novick

Mills & Boon Limited

London • Sydney • Toronto

Contents

GENERAL INTRODUCTION

It is the aim of this book to help you make use of your loom — not to teach you how to make a warp or to explain the different stitches — but to show you how you can use it to turn out articles of furnishing, clothing and decoration. In so doing — with the patterns provided — you will discover its technical possibilities for yourself.

Each pattern includes the heading 'materials', which gives the type and quantity of materials used. The same term can, however, refer to two very different types of wool, depending on the supplier (spinner, haberdashery shop, department store . . .), so look closely at the photograph of the finished product. This will show the thickness of the materials to be used.

Similarly the quantity given will only be valid for precisely that type of wool, yarn or cotton used, so it is best to use this as an approximate quantity and make sure that where necessary you will be able to buy more of the chosen yarn later. If not, buy an extra 100 g to be on the safe side.

When you have used this book for a while you will be able to make up new patterns yourself by either combining different elements from several patterns or by making up your own patterns.

If you use materials of a different thickness from that suggested, work from the diagrams which give the pattern in centimetres rather than from the text which gives the required number of threads, for you will need to change the number of threads.

Before you launch into weaving a particular article, make sure that your loom is wide enough to take it. Look first at the diagram which gives the measurements in centimetres; if any section is wider than the width of your reed you will be unable to make that particular article.

In almost every case instructions are given both for a very simple loom, called a 'table loom' and for a more elaborate loom, a 'four-shaft loom' (the shaft being the frame which holds the heddles). A few articles, however, can only be made if you have the latter type.

The table loom used here is one with an alternating reed; one with slot, hole, slot, hole, etc. alternately, with 4 dents to each centimetre (4 threads per cm). These looms are continuous warp looms. They have a warp beam at the back (roller of about 6 cm diameter) onto which you roll your reserve warp threads, and a cloth beam at the front, onto which the completed weaving is rolled.

With this 'continuous warp' facility the length of weaving is not restricted. You can make large seam-free articles of furnishing or, in the case of clothing, you can weave all the sections (fronts, back, sleeves, etc.) one after the other on threads of predetermined length.

There is another type of table loom, called a 'circular warp' loom. With this the length of the warp threads is restricted to the circumference of the frame, so that the size of the weaving is limited. Large pieces can only be made by joining separate

pieces together and when making a garment you will have to organise your weaving of different sections according to the length of warp available.

For example, you have a circular warp of 2 metres and you want to make a jacket with fronts 80 cm long, a back 76 cm long and sleeves 60 cm long. You will have to allow a 20 cm band of unwoven warp threads to allow you to cut between the separate sections and allow about 40 cm for shrinkage (for when the work is removed from the loom the threads contract considerably).

So first of all you wind a warp 54 cm wide onto the loom and with this first warp you weave the 80 cm fronts one after the other. You then leave a 20 cm band of unwoven threads and weave the first 60 cm sleeve. This will take up the whole length of warp. Cut these two sections, warp the loom again to a width of 50 cm and weave the 76 cm back and then the second sleeve, remembering to leave a 20 cm band unwoven. Certain similar operations occur repeatedly in the patterns. It would take too long to repeat them every time, so explanations of these different operations are given in numbered paragraphs at the beginning of the book.

You will find the titles of these paragraphs repeated at the beginning of each pattern and you will be reminded of them again at the appropriate moment in the course of your work.

1. MAKING A WARP

You have to make the warp (the threads which go lengthways over the loom) before attaching it to the loom. This ensures that it is the right length for the work you have in mind and that you have the right number of threads for the width.

E.g. you want to make a bolero. The diagram on page 51 shows that for size 76 cm bust the width should be 46 cm and the total length
26 + 26 + 22 + 26 = 100 cm.

You use 2 threads per cm, that is you thread two dents of the reed for every centimetre, so you multiply your width of 46 cm by 2, which gives 92 threads. The length of the warp is calculated by adding the lengths of the woven sections to the length of thread you will be unable to weave:

1. the length required for tying the threads to the warp beam.
2. the length of thread from the warp beam to the front of the reed, for when you come to the end of your weaving you will be unable to weave this section of the warp.
3. the length required for tying the threads to the cloth beam.
4. the length of the thread unwoven at the start (about 10 cm) in front of your finishing stitch. Leaving this gap prevents your first picks from becoming uneven where groups of warp threads are tied together onto the cloth beam.

All these unwoven sections add up to a loss of about 60 cm. So the length of your warp will be:
1 m + 0.60 = 1.60 m.

The warp can be made in different ways
—direct or sectionalised warping.
—indirect warping: using rotary, wall or table-mounted warp pegs or even between two chairs.

You should refer to a text book to find out how to use one or other of these warping processes.

2. PUTTING ON THE WARP

On both types of loom you have to centre your work, that is you have to make sure that your band of weaving is at the centre of the reed.

E.g.: your loom has a reed 80 cm wide with 4 dents per cm. You want to make the poncho (pattern no. 2) where the width is 70 cm. Leave 5 cm to both right and left, that is 5 cm x 4 dents per cm = 20 dents, the first thread will be threaded through the 21st space.

If your weaving is to be parallel it is important to centre it correctly.

(a) Table loom

It is merely a question of threading the warp through the alternating reed. This has slot, hole, slot, hole, etc. alternately, giving two slots and 2 holes per cm, that is 4 dents.

There are several ways of threading the warp. The basic rule is that a slot should always be followed by a hole, so that you always have a fixed thread (through the hole) followed by a moveable thread (through the slot—this thread is alternately lowered, when the reed is raised, and raised when the reed drops—it is this under-over movement which makes the weaving stitch).

Alternatively, depending on the ply of your weft, you can thread the warp at larger or smaller intervals or even at irregular intervals.

1. 4 threads per cm: the easiest way of using the reed is to thread every dent in order; if it has 4 dents per cm you will use 4 threads per cm. So you multiply the width of the weaving by 4 (see MAKING A WARP) to find the number of threads required for this width.

2. 2 threads per cm: to widen the space between your warp threads and to make your weft fuller you can use 2 dents per cm by threading one slot and one hole, missing one slot and one hole, etc.

Here you multiply the width by 2 to find the total threads needed.

3. 1½ threads per cm: when using unspun wool or fleece, the more your warp is spaced out, the more your weft will keep its fluffiness and softness. So you should space out your warp threads even more. Thread one slot, miss one hole and one slot, thread one hole, miss one slot and one hole, thread one slot, etc.

This gives 1½ threads per cm, so to get the total number of threads multiply the width by 1½.

4. More unusual patterns: it is impossible to list all the possible ways of threading the reed. Remember that you can thread two warp threads through some dents (preferably slots) to give a ribbed effect. You can thread two adjacent slots (missing the hole) then two adjacent holes (missing the slot) for a corrugated effect. You can thread one section with 4 dents per cm and follow by another with 2 dents per cm to aerate your weaving, etc. But if you put on the warp in any of these ways you will not get an even weaving stitch.

(b) Four-shaft loom
You must put on the warp in two steps: threading the reed and threading the heddles.

1. Threading the reed: reeds can range from 2 dents per cm to 24 dents per cm (or even more). The intervals between the threads depend on the thickness of your warp and weft yarns. This is indicated in the paragraph 'Making a warp' at the head of each pattern.

Thus, 'reed 2 dents per cm' indicates that you thread 2 dents per cm and that you have to multiply your width by 2 to find the number of threads required. 'Reed 4 dents per cm' shows that you need 4 threads per cm width; 'reed 6 dents per cm' that you need 6 threads per cm width, etc.

You do not need to buy the whole range of reeds in order to weave in different thicknesses, for each reed can be threaded in several ways. The simplest way to use the reed is to thread every dent, but you can also miss one or more dents between threads or equally well thread 2 threads into 1 dent.

For the articles in this book the ideal reed for your loom is a no. 4 reed (4 dents per cm).

This will allow you to weave:
—quite firm fabrics using every dent.
— softer fabrics, especially in mohair, using every other dent.
—more rustic fabrics using 1 dent in three.
—if you want to make very firm fabrics in cotton or linen you pass 2 threads through each dent (these 2 threads must, however, be separated into different heddles).

In the first instance you multiply by 4 to find the number of threads required for the width, in the second by 2, in the third by $1\frac{1}{2}$, in the last instance by 8.

2. Threading the heddles:
Traditional or serge pattern: this consists of distributing the threads in the order in which they come off the reed. The first thread goes into one heddle (metal needle with a central eye or fine cotton thread also with central hole) in the first shaft (frame to which the heddles are attached, the first shaft generally being the one closest to the reed and the fourth the one closest to the warp beam);
the 2nd thread in a heddle on the 2nd shaft
the 3rd thread in a heddle on the 3rd shaft
the 4th thread in a heddle on the 4th shaft
the 5th thread in a heddle on the 1st shaft
the 6th thread in a heddle on the 2nd shaft
the 7th thread in a heddle on the 3rd shaft
the 8th thread in a heddle on the 4th shaft
etc.

This method of threading the heddles is written as follows:
```
    4   4   4
  3   3   3
2   2   2
1   1   1
```

More unusual patterns: the traditional serge pattern is by far the most commonly used, but it limits the number of designs possible. It is almost impossible to count the number of more unusual patterns, they are so numerous. They are formed by arranging the threads irregularly through the shafts.

No matter how imaginatively the threads are distributed it is a good idea to have a thread through an odd number shaft followed by one through an even number shaft to ensure some kind of regular weaving stitch.

For example, chevron pattern:
```
      4   4
  3 3   3 3
  2   2 2   2
1   1   1
```

The threads are distributed as follows:
the first thread in a heddle on the 1st shaft
the 2nd thread in a heddle on the 2nd shaft
the 3rd thread in a heddle on the 3rd shaft
the 4th thread in a heddle on the 4th shaft
the 5th thread in a heddle on the 3rd shaft
the 6th thread in a heddle on the 2nd shaft
the 7th thread in a heddle on the 1st shaft
the 8th thread in a heddle on the 2nd shaft
etc.
or again:
```
          4 4
      3   3   3   3
    2 2 2   2 2 2
  1   1   1   1   1
```
1st thread shaft no. 1
2nd thread shaft no. 2
3rd thread shaft no. 3
4th thread shaft no. 2
5th thread shaft no. 1
6th thread shaft no. 2
7th thread shaft no. 3
8th thread shaft no. 4
9th thread shaft no. 1
10th thread shaft no. 4
11th thread shaft no. 3
12th thread shaft no. 2
etc.

NB: Once you have threaded the heddles you attach the threads to the warp beam. If this is 15cm or less in diameter it is essential to roll a sheet of strong paper (wrapping paper for example) onto the whole width of the beam with your warp threads, preferably the whole length of the warp, to preserve the regularity of successive layers of threads and to maintain an even tension. With a beam of larger diameter you can simply roll on your warp with no additional precautions.

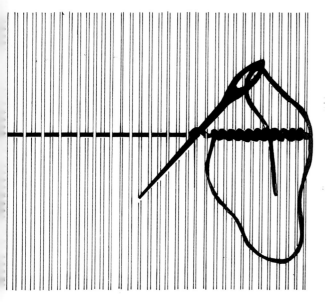

3. FINISHING STITCH

You will find this heading mentioned for each article and the finishing stitch may be used several times in the course of one pattern.

This stitch does not form a firm enough finish for you to be able to merely cut off your warp threads but it is useful as:
—a basis for your weaving.
—a tension guide.
—a temporary finishing.

(a) The stitch: make a plain weaving shed (it is immaterial whether the even threads are raised or dropped), pass your shuttle through the shed from right to left (from left to right if you are left-handed), cut off the thread on the shuttle leaving an end one and a half times longer than the width of the warp and release the shed so that you can work flat.

Take a large darning needle and thread it with the remaining length of weft thread.

Using this needle you are going to oversew the under warp threads with the weft. Insert your needle to the right of the under warp thread and above the last weft thread and bring it out below the weft thread and to the left of the under warp thread, so that the weft thread oversews the over warp thread. It is merely a question of looking for the next under thread without worrying about this over thread (see sketch).

(b) Finishing stitch used at the start of work: this row of stitching redistributes the warp threads, tied to the cloth beam in groups, to give an even first pick. To be effective it must be about 12 cm from the cloth beam.

It also serves to check tension. By bringing the reed up to this row of stitches and applying slight pressure (do not beat it down) you will see that any insufficiently tensioned threads become loose below the row of stitching. When you move the reed away again the untensioned threads will have formed waves and made your finishing stitch uneven. You must undo your joining knots and retension the threads one at a time (if you try to do them all together the tension will remain uneven) until the finishing stitches form an even line, parallel to the batten to which they are attached (cloth beam).

(c) Finishing stitch in the course of work: this stitch is used to finish neck or sleeve openings (it will keep the weft in position while you continue weaving). It is also used to finish shoulders of garments, each separate section of a garment, openings where you will insert voile and any cut-away sections in a decorative panel.

It is also used at the start of each new section.

(d) Finishing stitch at the end of a piece of work: this allows you to cut your woven sections 5 cm from the edge without needing to finish off with a fringe. It makes an excellent basis for the finishing process (see section on 'Finishing').

Remarks: When your finishing stitch goes right across the warp, you will be left with some thread in your needle. The remaining thread should be split and half of it woven into the following pick (the other half of the split thread can simply be cut off eventually). In the case of a finishing stitch at the end of a section of work or at a sleeve or neck opening you run this extra thread through the selvedge through the loops formed by the weft for about 3 cm.

At either the beginning or end of a piece of work use the weft thread on the shuttle to measure one and a half times the width of the warp and use this for your finishing stitch. For neck and sleeve openings which are finished at the same time as the shoulders there is no thread on the weaving for you to use. So use a separate piece of thread in your needle and sew it into the sleeve or neck selvedge for about 3 cm.

4. JOINING THE WEFT
The thread on the shuttle runs out:
work to the end of the shuttle, eventually weaving the last section of thread by hand. Split the last 3 cm of the thread into two. Leave half the thread woven into the warp and bring out the other half to the top side of the weaving at the start of the split. Reload the shuttle, again splitting the last 3 cm into two. Pass the shuttle through the shed in the same direction as the previous pick so that one half of the split thread overlaps the 3 cm of split thread from the last shuttle. Bring the other half to the top side of the weaving where the split begins.

This maintains the same thickness of weft at the join and leaves two short ends of split thread 3 cm apart. These threads can be cut off but it is best to leave this until the weaving is removed from the loom and has contracted fully.

It is not possible to split every yarn, mohair for instance, or cotton, for these have only one ply. These are simply overlapped without being split and since they are very fine the double thickness will not be noticeable.

Stripes or plaid: here you have to change colour quite often. If you are making a garment seamed at the edges you can start and finish each shuttle at the outside edge and leave them attached until the colour is required again. Any large loops formed by the threads running along the edge can be worked into the seams.

With an article where the selvedge edge will remain visible each completed band of colour will have to be finished off. Finish the strip at either edge, split 3 cm of wool, fold half back into the same shed as your last pick around the selvedge thread. Start a new colour at the opposite side with a new shed (this avoids overlapping threads at the same side which could make the weaving misshapen). Split the first 3 cm of wool on the shuttle and fold half into the first pick around the selvedge thread.

5. HOW TO MEASURE YOUR WORK
Lengths to be woven are generally greater than the distance between the cloth beam and the reed, so you will have to measure your work as you go along. Each time you measure tie a short length of wool to the selvedge thread and jot down the length to this point. Measure next from the previous piece of wool so that by adding the figures up as you go along you will know when you have reached the required length.

Then unroll the weaving and measure the whole length again. There will be a slight discrepancy between your addition sum and your final measurement. This arises from the fact that the warp is tensioned on the loom as far as the elasticity of the yarn will allow. When unrolled the warp retracts and returns more or less to the original length, causing the weaving to shrink slightly (it will not return completely to the original length, for some of the elasticity will have been lost).

This shrinkage is called 'flattening'. It works out to roughly 5 cm per metre, but will be different for different materials.

You will then have to weave the length necessary to give the required overall length.

6. MOHAIR WOOL
Although thought to be expensive, it is not expensive to use for it goes a long way. A whole jacket for a size 86.5 cm bust uses about 500 g of wool, a shawl 250 g. If you buy a good quality wool, with a lot of hair, it will scarcely compress at all.

You make a warp with your mohair (for this choose 2-ply mohair with a fibrous thread, for this is stronger) and then weave the weft. When you beat it down with the reed this should give equal squares between the warp and the weft. There should be a small square space left between two adjoining warp threads and two successive picks. This space will be visible because the reed flattens the fibres but when you have finished weaving the work will regain its softness by simply rubbing it against another piece of fabric or brushing with a soft brush. If the weaving is too compressed the mohair will felt with use.

7. UNSPUN WOOL
This comes in lengths, sometimes fine enough for light to pass through it, sometimes in a thick, dense length. The former can be used as it comes but the latter should be split into 4 or 5 thinner lengths.

If this wool is to retain its fullness and fluffiness you must leave considerable gaps between the warp threads. The ideal distribution being 1 to $1\frac{1}{2}$ threads per cm.

Unspun wool used alone

(a) four-shaft loom: we have seen in the section 'PUTTING ON THE WARP' how you should thread the reed if you are going to work solely with unspun wool. Take a no. 2 reed and thread each dent if you are using the fine lengths split into two or the thicker lengths split into 8 (child's jacket), or every other dent (1 thread per cm) when using the fine lengths as they come or thick strips divided into 4.

(b) table loom: as with the four-shaft loom, you can use very fine thread (child's jacket) by threading one slot and one hole, missing the next slot and hole, threading one slot and one hole, etc. If you use thicker lengths of unspun wool thread one slot, miss one hole and one slot, thread one hole, miss one slot and one hole, etc.

Unspun wool with other materials
In intricate work you can insert bands of unspun wool to create a contrast of materials (hooded jacket).

If your warp is too close together your unspun wool will be completely crushed:

(a) four-shaft loom: all you need to do to create sufficient space between the warp threads is to use one of the plain weave treadle combinations to give two threads over and two threads under. This combination (e.g. 1–4) can be the same for each band of unspun wool if you intersperse them with a few picks of plain weave. In this way your rows of unspun wool will be repeated at regular intervals. If you want two or more successive bands of unspun wool or to have them at irregular intervals, you should alternate the plain weave treadle combinations.

If your work is extremely fine (4 threads per cm or more) you must use unspun wool by pulling down 3 layers of threads (123 for example) if your loom is one that pulls down (that is if the movement made to separate the layers of threads lowers the shafts) or on the contrary by raising one layer of threads if your loom raises the shafts (if the movement made to separate the layers of threads raises the shafts). This will give 3 lowered threads to one raised one in the shed.

(b) table loom: you cannot use different sheds here, for the only stitch possible is plain weave, so you will have to space your threads yourself by hand.

You will have to re-divide the upper threads in the shed yourself by taking every other thread or one in three, depending on the spacing required (that is, you pass your unspun wool under the first thread, over the second, under the third, over the fourth, etc.).

You can weave your unspun wool through these upper threads of the shed in exactly the same way to get the material evenly distributed, but you will need several picks of plain weave between your picks of unspun wool.

If you wish to have two or more successive picks of unspun wool or to obtain an uneven effect use the two sets of threads in the shed alternately and where you have gone over threads in the first pick, go under them in the second.

Joining and finishing unspun wool

(a) if you want to make something entirely in unspun wool: measure a length of approximately three widths (the longer your wool, the more likely it is to break during weaving). You can break the wool by hand and tease out the ends to make joins less obvious. To start your first piece pass it through the upper threads of the shed by hand leaving about 2 cm at the beginning of the pick. Fold this into the first pick around the selvedge thread. When one length is finished take another and overlap the end of the previous thread. Since unspun wool is very fluffy these joins will not be noticed when beaten down.

(b) to weave several bands of unspun wool at intervals: tear off a length 4 cm longer than the width of the weaving. Pass this

wool through the shed by hand and turn in the 2 cm at either end around the selvedge thread, weaving them in with the first pick.

8. RAW WOOL OR FLEECE

(a) continuous use: that is with the small tufts of fleece used one after another (for this wool comes in small tufts), crossing 2 or 3 warp threads and passing through the same openings as those described for unspun wool.

(b) used as fleece: that is to recreate the look of lamb-skin. The tufts of wool are teased out by hand until light and fluffy. These are woven into picks of plain weave and pulled out slightly between the warp threads at regular intervals so that they fluff out. You could do this on every pick but this would give a very bushy fabric (almost too bushy for use as a garment). You should therefore intersperse it with a few picks of plain weave in the same wool or cotton used for the warp. This will not be visible under the fleece.

This type of weaving is quite fragile, in any case, and the tufts of fleece are likely to be pulled out. If you weave one pick with the shuttle loaded with the warp wool (or cotton) for each pick of fleece this will strengthen your weaving but will not be visible.

(c) spacing of the warp: when raw wool is used for continuous weaving the same rules of warp spacing apply as for unspun wool.

Used in fleece form the spacing can easily range from 2 to 6 threads per cm. If you have more than 6 threads per cm proceed as for unspun wool.

9. FABRIC WEAVING (LIRETTE)
This is the name given to an ancient weaving technique found in every civilisation. It involves using old fabrics to make new ones. These old fabrics must be supple, preferably cotton fabrics or jerseys, or even worn sheets which can be dyed bright colours to brighten up your weaving.

Cut strips about 2 cm in width. They should be cut with sharp scissors, for if you

tear them they will fray and make your weaving untidy.

The secret of beautiful fabric weaving is variety of colour and mixing plain and patterned fabrics, with the fabrics alternating often. Don't make your strips too long for this would make the areas of colour too large.

To start your first strip, cut the ends to a point, pass it through the shed by hand leaving about 3 cm at the start of the row. Turn the end round the selvedge thread and weave into the first row.

To join two strips overlap them for about 2 cm.

The correct spacing of the warp for fabric weaving is 2 dents per cm.

The fabric can be threaded into the eye of a large darning needle and used for the finishing stitch, but you can also start with a few picks of plain weave in the same yarn as the warp and use this yarn for the finishing stitch at the start and end of your work as well as on any neck or sleeve openings.

10. FINISHING
Always press your weaving initially with a steam iron or damp cloth.

Finishing off the warp threads

(a) If you have a sewing machine: the process will be simpler and much quicker. Sew all edges with a double zig-zag stitch if your machine has this facility or a triple row of straight stitch. You can then cut off all your warp threads close to this row of stitching.

(b) If you have no sewing machine: you will have to finish off your warp threads with a needle. This method takes longer but it gives an attractive finish and requires no further attention. To finish off in this way you need at least 5 to 8 cm of warp thread over at the end of each section. (This is why you leave 20 cm of warp unwoven between each section of weaving and cut through the centre of this band to separate them.)

Thread 4 threads at a time into the eye of a darning needle and sew them in parallel to a warp thread through 5 or 6 weft threads on the wrong side if the weaving is not reversible, or on what you have decided will be the wrong side after comparing flaws in the two sides.

Proceed in this way top and bottom, at sleeve and neck openings and shoulders (at neck openings sew in groups of threads to match the decreasing warp threads: e.g. 6-4-2, sew in the first 3 threads, then the next 3, then the 4 threads on the next decrease, then the last 2). The threads will still be a few centimetres too long and can be cut off.

Sewing garments together

The diagrams for each pattern generally show how to sew the sections together.

(a) If you have a sewing machine: join all seams with straight stitch. One row of stitching will be enough for 'natural selvedge' edges, those made on the loom. For zig-zagged or machined edges, like shoulders or sleeves, it is best to make a double row of stitching.

(b) If you have no sewing machine: sew all seams by hand using the yarn used for the warp and a very small stitch.

(c) To make the shoulders of garments flat: make a slight curve when sewing separate fronts and backs together. Start sewing right at the edge of the neck and continue in a straight line to about 2 cm below the edge at the sleeve opening.

Finishing off

(a) If the warp has been sewn in by hand: you can leave this as it is, for you already have a firm, strong finish, but you can use braid or a row of crochet to make it look better.

(b) If your finishing stitching has been machine done: you have to conceal the rows of stitching. This can be done either by making a small turn which will leave the sewing visible on the wrong side, or by making a real hem (turned twice). For revered sleeves make your turn or hem on the right side so that when the bottom of the sleeve is turned back the stitching will not be visible.

To flatten the edges down you can oversew all round the garment.

(c) Braid: you can buy cotton bias binding or woollen braid to go round the edges of your work in a haberdashery. This is an attractive form of finishing, and will help to reinforce the neck which might become misshapen. Bias binding is much used in this book. It can brighten up your weaving and can be most effective for articles made up from strips or squares of weaving where your loom is too small to make large articles all at one go.

Braid can be sewn around selvedge edges to hide stitching or sewn on flat when you want to decorate an edge sewn in by hand or hemmed.

If you want to hide seams with braid (see cashmere coat and skirt, man's sailor jacket, poncho) turn to the wrong side and braid any seams that are visible. This will give seams concealed by bias binding on the right side and a very neat finish on the wrong side.

(d) Crochet: it is also possible to conceal stitches or make edges more attractive with a row of crochet all the way round; a half-cable stitch is generally used. You can also make a tight garment fit better by crocheting a band to go under the arm hole or as a border for the two front openings.

(e) Fringes: you may decide to make the cut warp threads into a fringe around the bottom of an article of clothing or furnishing.

Once the line of stitching or zig-zag of the finishing stitch has been done the warp threads can be left as they are. Or they can be knotted immediately below the finishing stitch if you have no sewing machine, or if you wish to use the fringes to create a net-like effect as in the decorative panel. To make a fringe, take 4 threads, wrap them round your finger to make a loop, and slip the ends of the wool through the loop to make a knot.

In the case of the shawl or the Andes cape, two sides have no warp threads to form a fringe, so you have to add separate fringes. Measure the existing fringes, multiply by $2\frac{1}{2}$ and cut threads of this length. Take 2 threads at a time, fold in half, place crochet hook through selvedge, place the folded threads onto the crochet hook, pull through and push the 4 ends through the loop to make a knot.

Fastenings

(a) If you have a sewing machine which makes buttonholes: you can use it for your weaving, provided you weave very tightly, to make garments which cross over (man's sailor jacket). It is not possible to make button holes by hand for they would fray too quickly.

(b) Ties: these are particularly easy to make and allow edge to edge fastening. If you are using bias binding around a garment allow an extra 20 cm at either end (see bat-sleeve tunic), or you can sew 20 cm lengths of tape under your edging braid at regular intervals.

(c) Loops: these are used with buttons and so can give a very close fastening. They can be made with wool (naval jacket with shoulder buttons) or with bias binding folded in two and attached in the same way as the ties.

Beaded Shawl (1.20m × 1.20m)

Before starting see:
Finishing Stitch - Mohair Wool -
Fringes

MATERIALS: 300 g mohair, 1 reel thread to match, some unusual beads.

WARP: Shawls are too large to be made on a table loom, which will rarely be more than 1 m wide.

Four-shaft loom: Make a 240 thread warp, 2 m in length. Reed used has 2 dents per cm. Thread for serge pattern:

```
    4   4   4
  3   3   3
2   2   2
1   1   1        etc.
```

WEAVING: Start weaving 15 cm from your joining knots to allow for a good fringe.

Make your first pick of plain weave with the mohair and attach a thread 2.40 m in length to the end of it. This will be used for the finishing stitch and to sew in your beads at the required intervals. When you want to sew in a bead, thread it onto your needle and slide along the thread to the base of the plain weave, continue your finishing stitch as usual.

When the row of beads is completed, weave a 10 cm band of plain weave and finish with a second row of beads identical to the first. Leave a band of unwoven warp threads and start again with another row of beads. Weave a further 80 cm from this point and finish this band with a 4th row of beads. Leave another 10 cm band of unwoven warp and finish with a 10 cm band of plain weave, beginning and ending with a row of beads. This will give a square 1.20 × 1.20 m.

Cut off your work 15 cm beyond last row of finishing stitch.

TO MAKE UP: Use any left over mohair warp thread to make fringes for the two plain edges.

Fold the square in half diagonally—and it is ready to wear.

Poncho

Before starting see:
Finishing Stitch - Finishing

This poncho can be made on a small loom and with odments of wool in graduated colours. Since it is impossible to join the small bands imperceptibly, it is best to emphasise the seam rather than to try to conceal it. With this in mind the seam has been covered with three lengths of bias binding.

MATERIALS: 300 g country-style wool, wool oddments.

WARP: Make a 140 thread warp, 5.80 m in length using black country-style wool.

Table loom: Use a reed with 2 dents per cm; thread one slot and one hole, miss one slot and one hole, thread one slot and one hole, etc.

Four-shaft loom: use a reed with 2 dents per cm and thread for serge pattern:

```
        4   4   4
      3   3   3
    2   2   2
  1   1   1        etc.
```

WEAVING: Use plain weave.
Weave small stripes with no more than 10 picks in the same colour to make a band of 2.40 m.
   Leave a 40 cm band of warp unwoven, then weave a second band of 2.40 m.

TO MAKE UP: Remove the woven bands from the loom. Press them using a damp cloth or steam iron.
   Sew the two bands together leaving a slit about 32 cm long for the neck.
   Cover the seams and edge the neck opening with 3 lengths of bias binding to tone with your wool colours.
   The fringes can be left (see 'Fringes') or sewn in and the bottom of the poncho edged like the neck opening.

Camel-Hair

Before starting see:
Finishing Stitch - Finishing

MATERIALS: 600 g camel-hair wool

WARP: It is essential to use a large reed, which means that it is impossible to use a table loom, for the hole in the reed would be too small to take the thick wool. The reed should therefore have 2 dents per cm.

Make a warp of 60 threads for sizes 76 cm and 81.5 cm bust, and 64 threads for sizes 86.5 cm and 91.5 cm bust, 4.70 m in length (5 m for sizes 86.5 cm and 91.5 cm).

Thread the heddles in the following way:

```
    4   4   4
   3   3   3
  2   2   2
 1   1   1      etc.
```

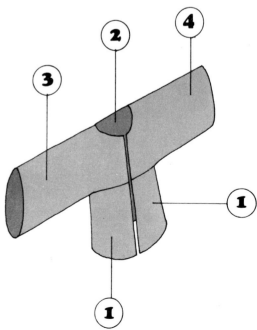

Blouson (To fit sizes 76 cm, 81.5 cm, 86.5 cm and 91.5 cm)

WEAVING: Use plain weave.
Weave a first band of 96 cm (103 - 110 - 117) for the body.

Leave 20 cm of warp unwoven so that you will be able to cut the sections easily when you have finished weaving.

Weave a second band of 1.20 m (1.23 m – 1.26 m – 1.29 m) for the back.

Leave 20 cm of warp unwoven.

Weave a third band (one bodice front). When it is 55 cm in length bring out the shuttle 22 threads (26 threads for sizes 86.5 cm and 91.5 cm bust) from the right-hand edge, go back towards the left. When you return to the right-hand side leave 2 more threads unwoven, go back towards the left. When you return to the right leave 2 more threads. Decrease 2 threads twice more.

You now have 30 threads (34) unwoven on the right-hand side, and 30 threads on the left on which you continue weaving until the total length is 64 cm (66 – 68 – 70).

Leave 20 cm of warp unwoven and make a second piece identical to the previous one for the second bodice front.

TO MAKE UP: Remove the weaving from the loom and cut between the sections in the centre of the unwoven warp.

With the machine sew a zig-zag or double line of straight stitch at each end of each section and around the neck opening. Cut your warp threads off short.

If you have no sewing machine sew in the unwoven warp threads one at a time on the wrong side using a large darning needle. They should be sewn in parallel with the warp through 3 or 4 picks.

Spread the back section (band of 1.20 m – 1.23 m – 1.26 m – 1.29 m) out flat and place the two front bodice sections on it edge to edge, with the straight edges outermost. The

two neck openings should meet at the centre of the back section.

Sew the back and front sections together along the top (neck edge). At the bottom sew together 38 cm from each end.

Fit the body on to the bodice by sewing your length of 96 cm (103 – 110 – 117) around the bodice starting at the selvedge edge of one of the fronts and continuing to the selvedge edge of the second front.

FINISHING: When you have made up the blouson knit a band of single rib (knit one, purl one) on no. 5 needles at the bottom of the sleeves and the body to gather up the weaving.

For the sleeves pick up 38 stitches (40) and rib 18 rows (20 – 22 – 24). For the body pick up 130 stitches (134 – 138 – 142) and rib 10 rows (12 – 14 – 16).

Edge the neck opening with dark brown bias binding (bought from a haberdashery) leaving 25 cm over at each end to form ties.

Bind the front edges in the same way, stopping at the top of the rib and leaving a

piece 25 cm long on each side for the ties.

Cover the seam between the body and bodice with a piece of binding placed flat, leaving 25 cm binding at each end.

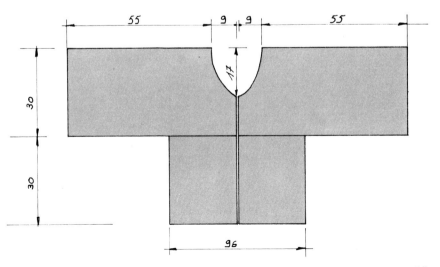

Blouse-Waisted Dress (To fit bust sizes 86.5–91.5 cm)

Before starting see:
Finishing Stitch - Finishing

MATERIALS: 500 g aubergine fine bouclé wool.

WARP: Make a warp 60 cm wide with 4 threads per cm, i.e. 240 threads, 3.20 m in length.

Table loom: use each dent.

Four-shaft loom: use a reed with 4 dents per cm and plain weave pattern:

```
        4   4   4
      3   3   3
    2   2   2
  1   1   1      etc.
```

WEAVING: Use plain weave.

Weave a length of 1.25 m, then take a second shuttle. With the left-hand shuttle weave 105 threads from the left-hand side, and with the right-hand shuttle weave 105 threads from the right-hand side (the shuttles should enter the shed from opposite directions). Do not weave the 30 threads left at the centre. Working both sides together decrease 6 threads on alternate rows, twice on the right-hand side of the neck opening and twice on the left (54 unused threads at the centre). Continue straight for 4 cm and then increase on alternate rows, increasing 1 thread each time until the two shuttles meet at the centre. Continue weaving for a further 10 cm on two shuttles to form a slit.

Remove one of the shuttles and continue weaving right across the warp with one shuttle for a further 1.10 m.

FINISHING: Remove from the loom and press with a damp cloth or steam iron.

For instructions on sewing in the threads turn to the 'Finishing' section.

Fold the length of weaving in two. Sew up each side to 25 cm below the fold (shoulder), leaving an opening in one side of 15 cm at the waist, which you can find in the following way.

Measure the length of the skirt (70 cm in this pattern) and thread through 2 draw-strings, drawing them up to fit your waist measurement and reinforcing them on the wrong side.

Sew a zip fastener into the side slit.

The bodice which is longer than the length from shoulder to waist will blouse out over the hips.

Before starting see:
Finishing Stitch - Finishing

Pinafore Dress (Any size)

MATERIALS: Knitting cotton, 50 g orange, 50 g golden yellow, 100 g sunshine yellow, 100 g straw yellow, 250 g écru (natural).

Waist-band tape: 1.50 m (5 cm wide)

Yellow, écru and orange braid: 5 m each.

WARP: Make a 300 thread warp, 2.50 m in length, distributing the bands of colour in any way you wish (do not use too much ecru, this is to be used for the weft).

Table loom: use all the dents in your reed.

Four-shaft loom: use a reed with 4 dents per cm and thread for plain weave:

```
    4   4   4
  3   3   3
2   2   2
1   1   1    etc.
```

WEFT: Use plain weave.

Skirt: weave the whole width of the warp until the work measures 1.40 m. Leave a 20 cm band of warp unwoven.

Bodice: cut off 60 threads on either side of the weaving, and continue weaving over a width of 40 cm until the work measures 20 cm.

FINISHING: Remove from the loom. Press with a damp cloth or steam iron.

Cut through the centre of your band of unwoven warp to separate the two sections. Turn to the Finishing section for how to finish off the warp threads.

Measure your waist and cut a length of waist-band tape to this length. Gather the skirt to the same length. Cover your waist-band tape with all three colours of braid leaving an extra 30 cm of each at each end to form ties.

Do not sew down the outside edges of the tape. These will be sewn down later to cover the seams joining the waist band to the skirt and bodice.

Sew the gathered skirt to the waist band, fold down the orange tape and sew down by hand.

Sew up the back seam of the skirt, stopping 12 cm below the waist band.

Cover a 20 cm length of waist-band tape with the 3 braids. Do not sew down the bottom edge of the bottom tape.

Fold the bodice in two widthways to make a square 20 cm × 20 cm.

Sew the edges together and fix the waist-band tape along one of the sides of the bodice. Turn and sew down the last piece of tape to conceal the seam.

Cut two 25 cm lengths of waist-band tape and cover each with 3 pieces of braid 1.50 m in length. The extra 1.25 m will make the straps of the dress and tie behind the neck.

Sew these two lengths of waist-band tape to the sides of the bodice as before.

Sew the bodice to the waist band, and sew down the last edge of braid to hide this last seam.

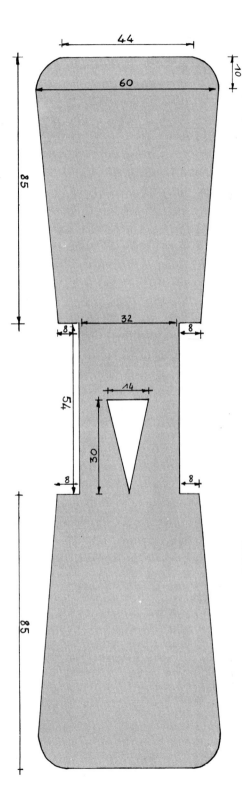

Tabard (One size, to fit

Before starting see:
Finishing Stitch - Mohair Wool -
Unspun Wool - Finishing

MATERIALS: 400 g mottled mohair wool, 25 g unspun wool.

WARP: Make a 120 thread warp, 3 m in length.

Table loom: use 2 dents per cm on your reed, that is, thread one slot and one hole, miss one slot and one hole, thread one slot and one hole, etc.

Four-shaft loom: Use reed with 2 dents per cm and serge pattern:

```
    4   4   4
  3   3   3
2   2   2
1   1   1   etc.
```

WEFT: Weave over the 88 centre threads, leaving 16 threads unwoven on either side.

Weave 4 picks, then increase 6 threads, weave 4 more picks and increase 6 threads again, 4 picks further on increase 2 threads, after a further 4 picks make your last increase of 2 threads.

Weave 4 picks and begin decreasing 1 thread at each side every 2 cm.

When the work measures 15 cm weave 5 picks of unspun wool at intervals, with 5 picks between each (see section 'Unspun Wool').

When the work measures 85 cm decrease 8 cm on each side for the sleeve openings, by leaving 16 threads on either side.

Weave on the 64 remaining threads for a further 24 cm and then begin the neck opening. Load a second shuttle. Use the first shuttle to weave the 18 threads on the

sizes 81.5 to 86.5 cm bust)

left, and the second for the 18 threads on the right (shoulders). This leaves 28 unwoven threads in the centre.

Pick up 1 thread every 2 cm at the neck edge with each shuttle.

After 30 cm you should have picked up all your threads. Continue weaving with one shuttle, picking up the 16 threads left on either side for the sleeves at the same time.

Pick up one thread on either side every 2 cm.

When you have picked up all 120 threads, weave 4 picks and then decrease 2 threads on each side; work 4 more picks and decrease 2 threads on each side; work 4 more picks and decrease 6 threads on each side; after 4 more picks decrease for the last time by 6 threads and end with 4 last picks.

Do not forget to include your picks of unspun wool symmetrically in the front.

Leave a 20 cm band of unwoven warp.

The pocket: Cut off 20 threads on either side so that you are weaving over a width of 40 cm. Make a rectangle 20 cm long for your kangaroo pocket.

FINISHING: Remove from the loom, press with a damp cloth or steam iron, turn to the section 'Finishing' for how to finish off the warp threads.

Sew black bias binding around the edge of the tabard, neck opening and pocket. Sew on the pocket 40 cm below the point of the neck opening.

Before starting see:
Finishing Stitch - Finishing

MATERIALS: Knitting cotton, 250 g khaki, 100 g pink, 100 g blue, 100 g ecru

WARP: Make a 166 thread warp, 5 m in length, arranging your colours as follows: 26 pink threads + 8 khaki + 10 pink + 4 ecru + 18 khaki + 16 blue + 12 pink + 16 khaki + 4 pink + 22 blue + 6 ecru + 24 pink = 166 threads.

Table loom: use each dent of the reed to a width of 40 cm.

Four-shaft loom: use reed with 4 dents per cm and thread the heddles in the serge pattern:

```
      4    4    4
    3    3    3
  2    2    2
1    1    1      etc.
```

WEAVING

Pinafores: weave a 54 cm band in khaki and oversew the two ends with finishing stitch (see 'Finishing Stitch'). Leave a 20 cm band of warp unwoven and weave a second 54 cm length. Leave another 20 cm unwoven.

Striped Bat-Sleeved Tunic (One size, 81.5 cm bust to fit 91.5 cm bust)

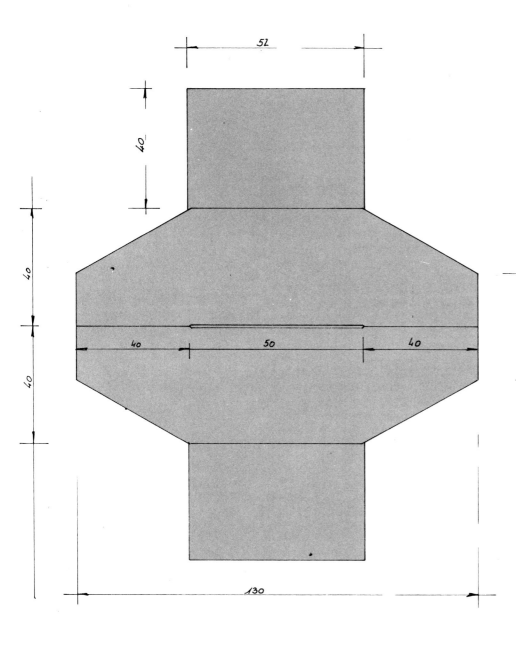

Bodices: count off 72 threads on the right-hand side and pass the shuttle through these 72 threads, finish them with finishing stitch. Increase one thread on the left-hand side every 4 picks, until you have picked up all the warp threads. This should give a length of about 40 cm (if necessary work a few more picks until you reach this length, if your weaving is longer than 40 cm, your sleeve will be slightly too long).

Weave 50 cm using the whole width of the warp, then decrease as you increased, that is, decreasing 1 thread on the left-hand side every 4 picks, finishing off with 72 threads.

Leave 20 cm warp unwoven and weave a second identical band.

TO MAKE UP: Remove from loom. Press, cut through the unwoven sections at the centre to separate the pieces of weaving.

Place the two bodice sections with straight edges together, and sew the straight edges together leaving a slit of 32 cm at the centre (neck opening). Open out and sew the two pinafore sections to the 50 cm edges in the middle of the bodice sections, leaving 2 cm at either side.

Fold right sides together and sew the bottoms of the bat-wing sleeves together. The sides of the tunic are not sewn.

Bind the neck opening and the cuffs, leaving 20 cm at either end so that you can gather in the sleeves.

Sew tape to the bottoms of the tunic too, leaving 40 cm of tape at either end for ties.

Repeat on the seam joining the pinafore to the bodice.

Before starting see:
Finishing Stitch - Finishing

MATERIALS: 400 g ecru linen yarn, 300 g red linen, 20 g lamé thread

WARP: Make a 278 thread warp, 4.20 m in length, distributing the colours as follows: 38 ecru threads, 2 lamé threads, 38 red, 2 lamé, 38 ecru, 2 lamé, etc.

Table loom: use all the dents in the reed.

Four-shaft loom: use a reed with 4 dents per cm and plain weave pattern:

```
 4   4   4
  3   3   3
 2   2   2
1   1   1     etc.
```

Front: Use plain weave.

Using the whole width of the warp, weave 20 picks in ecru, 2 picks lamé, 38 picks red, 2 picks lamé, 38 picks ecru, 2 picks lamé, 38 picks red, 2 picks lamé. Continue weaving alternately 38 picks ecru and 2 picks lamé.

When the work measures 54 cm, leave 20 threads on either side for the sleeve openings and load a second shuttle. Use the first to weave the 99 threads on the left, and the second for the 99 threads on the right, leaving 40 threads in the centre.

When you have woven 16 cm in this way begin decreasing for the neck, decreasing at each pick on the neck edge: 14 threads, 10 threads, 8 threads, 4 threads, 2 threads, 2 threads, with both shuttles.

Continue weaving on the 54 shoulder threads until the work measures 26 cm from the sleeve opening.

Leave a 20 cm band unwoven.

Back: Cut off 19 threads from either side of the warp, to leave only 220 threads. Weave these in a check pattern identical to the first piece. When the work measures 54 cm leave 20 threads on either side for the sleeve openings and weave a further 24 cm on the remaining 180 threads.

Leave a 20 cm band unwoven.

Linen Tunic
(One size, to fit 81.5 cm to 91.5 cm bust)

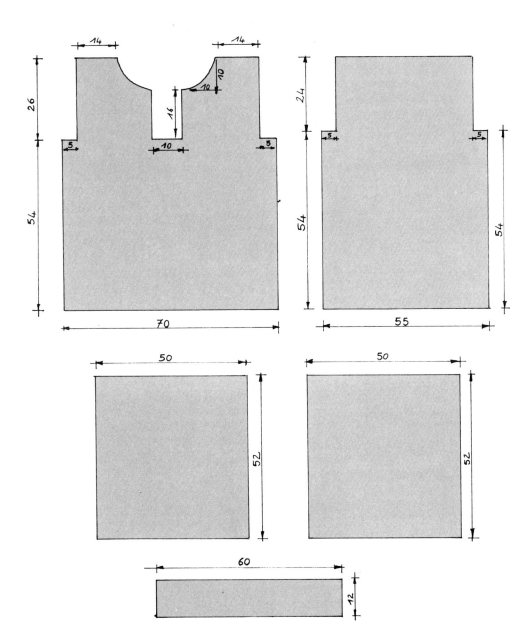

Sleeves: Cut off 10 threads on either side, leaving 200 threads. Weave a length of 52 cm in ecru.

Leave 20 cm warp unwoven.

Weave a second identical rectangle for the second sleeve.

Collar: Leave 20 cm unwoven warp and weave a length of 12 cm in ecru.

FINISHING: Remove from loom, press with a steam iron or damp cloth, cut the sections through the centre of the unwoven warp and turn to 'Finishing' section for how to sew in the ends of the warp.

Sew back and front shoulders together.

Open out flat.

Place the sleeves into the sleeve openings.

Fold over the 10 cm at centre front (unwoven band of threads) to give a flat fold.

Fix in place with two narrow seams at either side.

Fold the collar in two, and sew around neck.

Hem the bottom of the tunic and sleeves.

Before starting see:
Finishing Stitch - Mohair Wool -
Unspun Wool - Finishing

MATERIALS: Mohair wool (2 colours, 125 g light-coloured mohair, 375 g dark); 150 g unspun wool (3 colours).

WARP: Make a 120 thread (124 – 128) warp, 5 m (5.10 m – 5.20 m) in length.

Table loom: use your alternating reed, threading one large slot and one small hole; missing one slot and one hole; threading one slot and one hole; missing one slot and one hole . . .

Four-shaft loom: use no. 2 reed (2 dents per cm) and thread for serge:

```
    4    4    4
   3    3    3
  2    2    2
 1    1    1    etc.
```

Use all the light-coloured mohair and part of the dark for the warp, distributing the colours as you wish.

WEAVING: In dark-coloured mohair only.

Back + fronts: the body of the jacket is made in one piece.

Begin with the back by weaving a 70 (72 – 74) cm band of plain weave, inserting a pick of unspun wool every 20 picks (see section on weaving with unspun wool). Use one colour unspun wool only to avoid difficulties in matching the fronts.

When the work is the required length, load a second shuttle to weave the two shoulders on either side of the neck opening. Your two shuttles should enter the shed from opposite directions. Leave 28 (30 – 32) threads at the centre and weave the 46 (47 – 48) remaining threads on the two outside edges at the same time to a length of 12 cm. Then increase gradually at the centre on each pick for each side: 1 thread (2 threads for sizes 86.5 cm and 91.5 cm bust), then 2 threads (3 threads for sizes 86.5 cm and 91.5 cm bust), 4 threads and six threads.

Your two shuttles should now pass through all the warp threads and be at the centre. Weave the two opposite fronts until they measure 60 cm from the last increase, adding picks of unspun wool at any interval and in whatever colour you like.

Leave 20 cm warp unwoven.

Hooded Jacket (To fit bust sizes 81.5 cm, 86.5 cm and 91.5 cm)

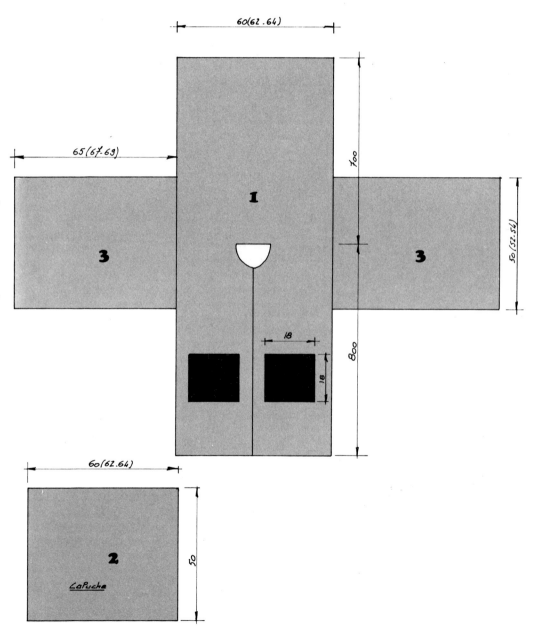

Hood: Weave a 50 cm length the same width as the body of the jacket, alternating the plain weave with a few picks unspun wool.

Leave 20 cm warp unwoven.

Sleeves: The sleeves are narrower than the other sections, so 10 cm from the warp width will not be used, that is 5 cm at each side so that the weaving will remain centred. You have 2 warp threads per cm, so cut off 10 threads on either side (5 cm × 2 threads = 10 threads).

Weave your first sleeve to a length of 65 cm (67 – 69) adding picks of unspun wool as you wish, but making a note of the distribution so that you can weave your second sleeve to match.

Leave 20 cm warp unwoven.

Weave your second sleeve and again leave 20 cm warp unwoven.

Pockets: cut off 20 threads at the centre of the warp, leaving 40 threads on either side. Weave these simultaneously with 2 small shuttles until 20 cm in length to give your two pockets.

TO MAKE UP: All the sections of your jacket are now finished; cut off the warp 15 cm beyond your pockets.

Press, without separating the sections, with a damp cloth or steam iron.

Separate the sections by cutting through the centre of the unwoven warp and sew in the warp threads (see 'Finishing').

Lay the body of the jacket out flat, position the sleeves with the centre of the sleeve at the centre of the body and sew them on preferably by machine, or by hand using a very small straight stitch.

Fold the jacket over across the shoulders with right sides together and on the wrong side sew the bottoms of the sleeves and the sides together in one continuous row of stitching..

Fold the hood in two along the length of 60 (62 – 64) cm and sew up one of the 30 (31 – 32) cm sides. Sew the other 60 cm side around the neck opening, gathering it slightly.

Sew on the pockets at the required height and turn back the sleeves, sewing cuffs them down by hand.

Naval Jacket (To fit bust sizes 81.5 cm, 86.5 cm and 91.5 cm)

Before starting see:
Finishing Stitch - Finishing

MATERIALS

Warp: 300 g country-style wool

Weft: 400 g fine bouclé wool, white-blue-grey

WARP: Make a warp of 108 (112 – 116) threads, 4 m in length.

Table loom: thread 2 dents per cm, that is thread one slot and one hole, miss one slot and one hole, thread one slot and one hole, etc..

Four-shaft loom: Use reed with 2 dents per cm and plain weave pattern:

```
    4    4    4
  3    3    3
2    2    2
  1    1    1    etc.
```

WEAVING: Use plain weave.

Front: weave a length of 50 cm using the whole width of the warp. When the work is the required length leave 12 threads on either side for the sleeves and continue weaving on the 84 (88 – 92) centre threads. After 14 cm load a second shuttle: use the left-hand shuttle to weave 24 threads on the left-hand side and the other shuttle to weave 24 threads on the right-hand side. This leaves 28 (32 – 36) unwoven threads in the centre. Weave a further 14 cm and the front is finished.

Leave 20 cm warp unwoven.

Back: cut off 2 threads on either side of the warp. Weave a length of 50 cm, then leave 12 threads at either side and weave on the 80 centre threads (84 – 88) for a further 24 cm.

The back is finished; leave 20 cm unwoven warp.

Sleeves: for size 81.5 cm keep all the threads, for size 86.5 cm cut off 2 warp threads on either side, for size 91.5 cm, cut off 4 threads on either side.

Weave 2 rectangular sections, 50 cm in length, leaving 20 cm unwoven warp between them.

The weaving is finished; cut the warp and remove from loom.

FINISHING: Press with a damp cloth or steam iron and cut through the middle of the unwoven warp to separate the sections. Finish off the warp threads as described in the section 'Finishing'.

Place back and fronts together so that the front shoulders overlap the back by 2 cm and pin together.

Open out and lay flat. Fit sleeves in sleeve openings.

Fold the jacket and on the wrong side sew the underside of the sleeves and the sides together one after the other, finishing 12 cm from the bottom to leave side slits on the hips.

Turn the jacket to the right side, remove the pins from the shoulders. Make button loops on the front shoulders and sew buttons onto the back.

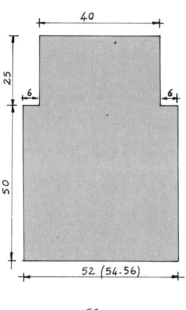

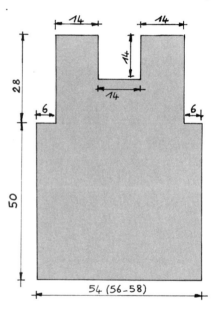

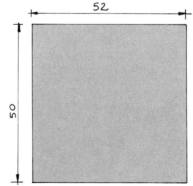

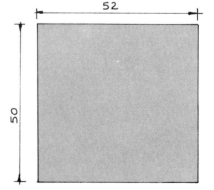

Mohair Kimono (To fit bust sizes 81.5 cm, 86.5 cm and 91.5 cm)

Before starting see:
Finishing Stitch - Mohair Wool -
Finishing

MATERIALS: 500 g grey mohair wool, 100 g wine-coloured mohair

WARP: Make a first warp of 128 (132 – 136) threads, 3.60 m in length, alternating the colours in the following way: 9 (11 – 13) wine threads, 20 grey, 10 wine, 20 grey, 10 wine, 20 grey, 10 wine, 20 grey, 9 (11 – 13) wine.

Table loom: use 2 dents per cm, that is, one slot and one hole, miss one slot and one hole, thread one slot and one hole, etc.

Four-shaft loom: use reed with 2 dents per cm and thread for plain weave:

$$\begin{matrix} & 4 & & 4 & & 4 \\ & & 3 & & 3 & & 3 \\ & & 2 & & 2 & & 2 \\ & 1 & & 1 & & 1 & & \text{etc.} \end{matrix}$$

WEAVING: Use plain weave. Grey mohair is used for the weft.

Fronts: divide your warp into two: 64 (66 – 68) threads on the right and the same on the left. Finish each front with a separate finishing stitch and weave with 2 shuttles, entering the first shed from opposite directions, so that decreases and increases will lie opposite one another.

Decrease one thread at each outside edge every 6 cm until the width is 50 cm (25 cm for each front); about 8 decreases.

At this point pick up all the outside threads in one pick with the appropriate shuttle.

You must now begin decreasing for the neck, decreasing 1 thread every 1.5 cm at each inside edge. When you have woven 25 cm from the neck opening you should have decreased 16 threads on each front.

When this section is 25 cm long finish the shoulders with finishing stitch and also the underside of the arms. The diagonal decreases can be left as they are. Leave 20 cm unwoven warp so that you will eventually be able to separate the sections.

Back: cut off 8 warp threads on either side to leave 112 (116 – 120) threads.

Make a line of finishing stitch across the whole width of the warp and with one shuttle weave a length of 50 cm, decreasing one thread at each side every 6 cm.

When the work measures 50 cm, pick up all the warp threads and weave a further 25 cm. Finishing stitch the top and under the arms. Leave 20 cm unwoven warp.

Sleeves: cut off 6 (8 – 10) threads on either side of the warp to leave 100 threads.

Oversew the whole width with finishing stitch and weave a 40 cm length. Finishing stitch this first sleeve.

Leave 20 cm warp unwoven.

Weave a second sleeve identical to the first.

Leave 20 cm warp unwoven.

Pockets: keep 80 warp threads and with 2 shuttles weave 2 squares 20 cm x 20 cm.

Cut the warp and remove from loom.

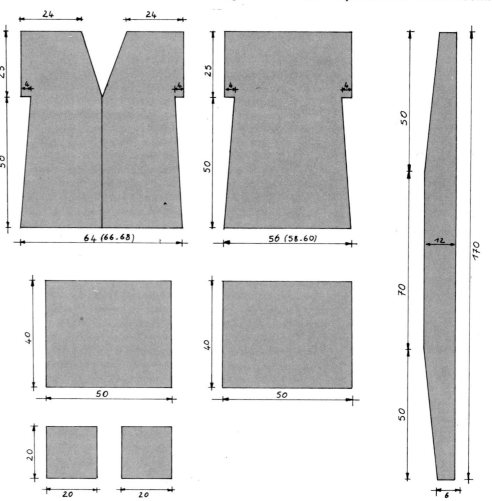

Lamé-Striped Tunic (One size, to fit 81.5 cm to 91.5 cm bust)

Collar: make a second warp 12 cm wide, that is with 24 threads, and 2.30 m long in grey.

Oversew the 12 right-hand threads with finishing stitch and begin by weaving only these 12 threads for 6 cm. Increase 1 thread, weave 4 cm, increase again; continue increasing in this way every 4 cm until you have picked up all the threads (12 increases).

Weave a further 70 cm on the whole width and then decrease in the same way as you increased, that is, one thread every 4 cm, finishing with a length of 6 cm woven on 12 threads.

Weave this section slightly more tightly than the rest of the work, so that your collar will keep its shape better.

FINISHING: Press and cut pieces through centre of unwoven warp.

Sew back and front shoulders together.

Place jacket flat and fit sleeves into shoulders.

On the wrong side sew together the underside of the sleeves and the sides, ending 10 cm from the bottom.

Measure the centre of the neck on the back and mark with a pin. Fold the collar in half and mark with a pin. Place the two pins one upon the other and sew the straight edge of the collar to the edges of the neck opening and the fronts of your jacket.

The collar should be slightly longer than each front. Once you have turned the collar to the right side and pressed it, fold these extra pieces to the wrong side and sew down to keep your collar nice and flat. For finishing off the warp threads and final finishing see 'Finishing'.

Before starting see:
Finishing Stitch - Finishing

MATERIALS: 300 g ecru cotton, 100 g bright turquoise bouclé cotton, 50 g pink lamé.

WARP: 280 warp threads, 1.80 m in length. The ecru cotton and bouclé are used together to form one warp thread.

Table loom: use every dent.

Four-shaft loom: use a **reed** with **4 dents** per cm and thread for serge pattern:

```
    4   4   4
  3   3   3
2   2   2
1   1   1    etc.
```

WEAVING: Use plain weave, alternating 20 picks single ecru cotton, 5 picks ecru cotton and lamé together, 15 picks ecru cotton and bouclé together, 5 picks ecru cotton and lamé together, then again 20 picks ecru cotton, etc.

Begin the back with a line of finishing stitch and work straight until the work measures 56 cm.

Then use **2** shuttles (you need 2 shuttles for each stripe): use the right-hand shuttle to weave the 108 threads which form the right shoulder. With the left hand shuttle weave the 108 threads of the left shoulder, until both measure 6 cm. This leaves 64 threads for the neck (which should be edged with finishing stitch) which you pick up gradually, increasing 1 thread every 0.5 cm.

When you have picked up all the threads, begin weaving across the whole width again until the work measures 1.20 m total length.

Finish with finishing stitch. Cut the warp 15 cm beyond this point.

FINISHING: Press with a damp cloth or steam iron.

To strengthen the edges oversew your 2 rows of finishing stitch with a single row of zig-zag or straight stitch on the sewing machine. If you have no sewing machine, knot your threads together 4 at a time to make a firm fringe.

Even out the fringes on the back and front and sew in the neck opening threads on the wrong side (see 'Finishing off the warp threads'). Sew braid to the edge of the neck opening and all round side edges of the tunic with 4 short ties on each side.

Man's Sailor Jacket

Before starting see:
Finishing Stitch - Finishing

MATERIALS: 500 g beige mottled wool,
500 g dark brown mottled wool

WARP: Make a 240 thread warp 5 m in
length, alternating, 1 dark brown thread, 1
beige—5 times—and, 1 beige thread, 1
dark brown—5 times.

Table loom: use all the dents in your reed.

Four-shaft loom: use reed with 4 dents per
cm and serge pattern:

```
        4    4    4
      3    3    3
    2    2    2
  1    1    1      etc.
```

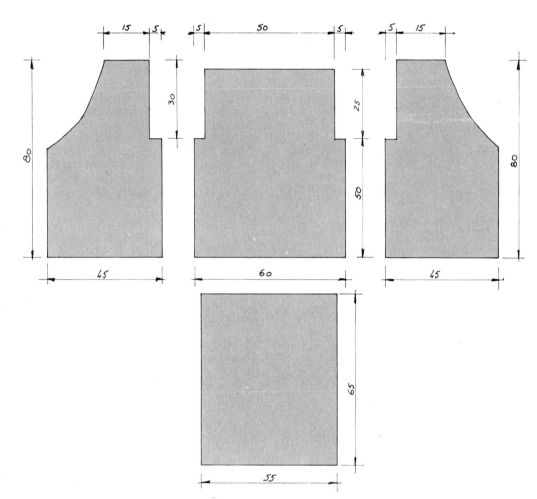

WEFT: Use plain weave.
   Load one shuttle with dark brown
mottled wool and one with beige and
weave, 1 pick dark brown, 1 pick beige—5
times—and, 1 pick beige, 1 pick dark
brown—5 times.

Back: Weave a length of 50 cm over the
whole width of the warp, alternating
shuttles as you weave. Leave 20 threads on
either side for sleeve openings, and finish
the back by weaving a further 25 cm on
the remaining 200 threads.
   Leave 20 cm warp unwoven.

Sleeves: With alternating shuttles weave 2
rectangles, 55 cm wide (cut off 10 threads
on either side to narrow the warp, and
weave on 220 threads) and 65 cm long.
   Leave a band of warp unwoven between
the two sections.

Fronts: Cut off 20 threads at either side.
Weave a length of 40 cm and begin
decreasing for the neck: on the right-hand
side decrease 1 thread every 0.5 cm to the
end.
   When the work measures 10 cm from the
first decrease, leave 20 threads on the left-
hand side for the sleeve opening and weave
a further 30 cm.
   Leave 20 cm warp unwoven. Weave a
second front identical to the first.

FINISHING: Remove weaving from loom,
press with damp cloth or steam iron. Cut

through the unwoven warps to separate the
sections and turn to the section 'Finishing'
for how to finish off the threads.
   Sew the front and back shoulders
together; place your weaving flat and sew
the sleeves into the sleeve openings.
   Sew the underside of the sleeves and
sides together with one continuous line of
stitching.
   Braid all the edges (front, neck, back,
sleeves, etc.).
   Make small loops with the braid to form
buttonholes.
   Sew on 3 buttons to match the loops and
3 corresponding buttons on the other front
to give a double-breasted effect.

Man's Shepherd-Look Waistcoat (one size)

Before starting see:
Finishing stitch - Fabric Weaving - Raw Wool - Finishing

MATERIALS

Warp: 200 g cotton.

Weft: 350 g Sardinian fleece, ecru; ecru fabric strips.

WARP: 140 threads, 2.50 m in length.

Table loom: use 2 dents per cm in your reed.

Four-shaft loom: use no. 2 reed and serge pattern:

```
    4   4   4
  3   3   3
2   2   2
  1   1   1      etc.
```

WEAVING: The weaving is made by alternating bands of fabric with bands of 5 picks fleece (see 'Fleece' and 'Fabric weaving').

Fronts: divide your warp into two sections with 70 threads to each, which are woven simultaneously from opposite directions.

Sew a row of finishing stitch with a strip of fabric or with your warp cotton (three strands) separately for each front and then weave 10 picks with fabric, followed by 5 picks of fleece, then another 10 picks of fabric, starting your first pick of fabric at the inside edge of the fronts so that the end of your 10th pick will also be at the inside edge. By weaving in this way and cutting off your fabric 30 cm from the edge of the weaving you make the ties (to strengthen the ties you can weave an extra strip of fabric across the whole width of the front, and leave 30 cm over on this strip too).

Continue weaving in this way until the work measures 50 cm, when you have to decrease for the arm hole. Leave 12 threads (6 cm) on the right-hand side of the right front and on the left-hand side of the left front.

Continue weaving on the 58 remaining threads up to the neck, i.e. 16 cm. Then decrease gradually on the inside edge of each front: 10 threads, then 8, then 6, then 2. You now have 32 threads for each shoulder. Continue weaving on these threads until the work measures 30 cm from the arm hole.

Your decreases will be stronger if they are done on the fabric picks, so you will have to vary the intervals of the decreases slightly to accommodate this.

Finish off the arm holes, neck and shoulders.

Leave 20 cm warp unwoven.

Back: Cut off 5 warp threads on either side to reduce the width of the back to 65 cm.

Begin the back with a row of finishing stitch and alternate picks of fabric and fleece as on the fronts.

When the work measures 50 cm leave 12 threads on either side for the arm holes, and weave a further 25 cm. Finish the top and arm holes.

FINISHING: Remove the weaving from the loom. It is not necessary to press it.

Oversew your rows of finishing stitch with a triple zig-zag or 3 rows of straight stitch, cut off the warp threads and turn the edges.

If you have no sewing machine, sew in the threads on the wrong side.

Sew the back and front shoulders together and sew up the sides.

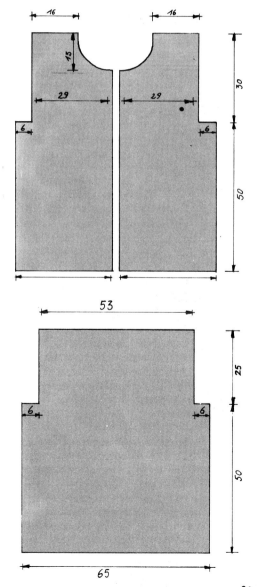

Fitted Skirt (Any size)

Before starting see:
Finishing Stitch - Finishing

MATERIALS: about 600 g cashmere wool (according to size); coloured braid

HOW TO MAKE YOUR PATTERN:
Measure your waist and hips.
  e.g.: Waist: 60 cm
        Hips: 90 cm.

Divide these two measurements by 4 (4 skirt panels).
  e.g.:$60 \div 4 = 15$ cm
       $90 \div 4 = 22.5$ cm

Measure the length between your waist and hips.

Take a sheet of newspaper or brown paper and fold it in two.

Take one quarter of your waist measurement and add 4 cm for seams.
  e.g.: $15 + 4 = 19$.
  Starting from the fold measure a width of 9.5 cm onto your sheet of paper ($19 \div 2 = 9.5$).
  28 cm below this line, measure the hip width + 4 cm.
  e.g. $22.5 + 4 = 26.5$. Divide this by 2 ($\frac{1}{2}$ on each side of the fold) $26.5 \div 2 = 13.25$.

Measure the length of the skirt and cut the paper at this length + 2 cm for the hem.
  e.g.: $75 + 2 = 77$ cm.

Take a ruler or long rod and draw a diagonal line through the end of the waist and hip lines to finish at the opposite end of the paper. Cut out the paper double along the diagonal, unfold it and you have the pattern for your skirt panel.

WARP: Measure the width of the bottom of your panel, e.g. 42 cm.
  Multiply this number by 4 (number of threads per cm), e.g. $42 \times 4 = 168$ threads.
  For the length of the warp, add the length of the first panel + 20 cm unwoven warp between panels + 2nd panel + 20 cm unwoven warp + 3rd panel + 20 cm unwoven warp + 4th panel + 60 cm total loss, e.g. $77 + 20 + 77 + 20 + 77 + 20 + 77 + 60 = 428$ cm (rounded up to 430 cm).

Table loom: use every dent in your reed.

Four-shaft loom: Use reed with 4 dents per cm and serge pattern:

```
        4   4   4
      3   3   3
    2   2   2
  1   1   1    etc.
```

WEFT: Use plain weave stitch.
  Weave about a dozen picks and pin your paper pattern to the base of the weaving.
  Stop weaving any threads which lie outside the edge of your pattern.
  Follow the edge of the paper, pinning it all along your panel as you go, and stop weaving any threads as soon as they fall outside it.
  When the first panel is finished, unroll it from the cloth beam to recover the pattern.

Wind it on again, leave 20 cm warp unwoven and proceed in the same way for the other 3 panels, remembering to separate each one by 20 cm unwoven warp.

FINISHING: When the 4 panels are finished, remove from loom, press with damp cloth or steam iron, cut through the centre of the unwoven warp to separate the panels and turn to 'Finishing' section for how to finish off the threads.

Sew the 4 panels together, leaving an opening 12 cm in length between 2 panels at the waist. Fit onto waist-band tape (about 3 cm wide) and cover with 2 lengths of binding, leaving 30 cm extra at either end (either side of the opening) for ties.

Turn to the wrong side and braid the seams and hem with the same bias binding.

Cashmere Coat (One size, to fit 81.5 cm to 91.5 cm bust)

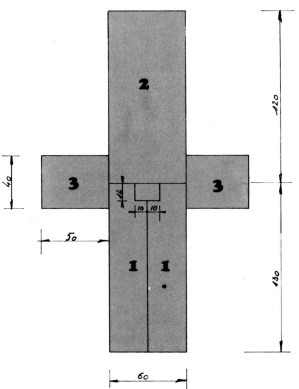

MATERIALS: 800 g cashmere wool, coloured tape.

WARP

Table loom: Make a warp of 280 threads, 4.30 m in length. Use 4 dents per cm, i.e. every dent in the reed.

Four-shaft loom: Make a warp of 280 threads, 4.50 m in length. Use reed with 4 dents per cm and thread heddles with serge pattern:

$$
\begin{array}{cccc}
 & 4 & 4 & 4 \\
 & 3 & 3 & 3 \\
 & 2 & 2 & 2 \\
 & 1 & 1 & 1 & \text{etc.}
\end{array}
$$

WEAVING

Fronts: Load 2 shuttles with cashmere thread used in one thickness (as it comes) and use them to weave 2 lengths each of 140 threads. These lengths make up the fronts.

Take care to keep the 2 shuttles opposite one another so that your decreasing for the neck will coincide on each front.

When the work measures 1.16 m leave 40 threads on each section at the centre for the neck opening.

Weave the remaining 100 threads on either side for a further 14 cm to make the shoulders of your coat.

Leave 20 cm warp unwoven.

Back: The back is only 60 cm wide, so cut 10 cm of warp threads, 5 cm on the right-hand side and 5 on the left (ie. 20 threads on either side, 4 × 5). Weave a large rectangle, 1.20 m in length for the back.

Leave 20 cm unwoven warp.

Sleeves: As the sleeves are 50 cm wide, proceed as for the back. Cut off 20 threads on either side to reduce the warp by 10 cm.

Weave a first rectangle, 40 cm in length, leave 20 cm unwoven warp and weave a second identical rectangle.

This makes your two sleeves.

Cut off your weaving.

FINISHING: Press the sections without separating them, then cut between the sections.

Sew the sections together leaving the bottom 60 cm of the side seams open.

Sew coloured braid along each edge and on the back of your seams.

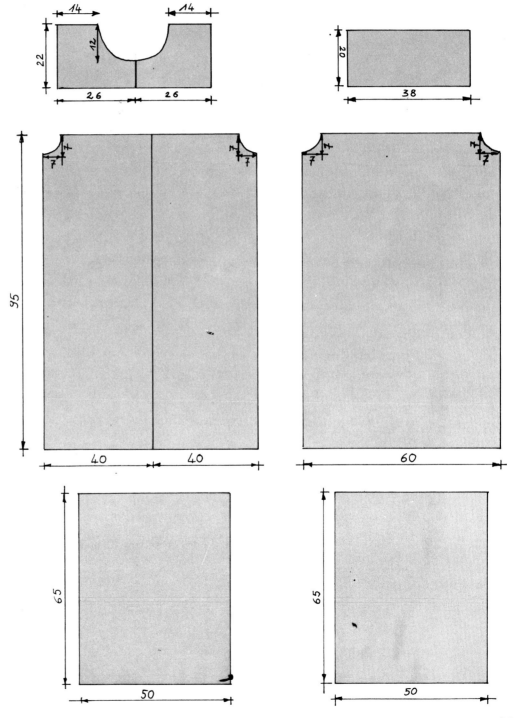

Mohair Coat (One size, to fit 86.5 cm to 91.5 cm bust)

Before starting see:
Finishing Stitch - Finishing -
Mohair Wool

MATERIALS: 700 g jasper, garnet-red and green mohair wool
150 g bronze mohair wool
100 g navy mohair wool.

WARP: Make a warp 80 cm wide with 2 threads per cm, i.e. 170 threads, 5.20 m in length, in the following order: 4 navy threads, 10 jasper, 6 bronze, 4 navy, 16 jasper, 6 bronze, 4 navy, 6 bronze, 48 jasper, 6 bronze, 4 navy, 6 bronze, 4 navy, 6 bronze, 16 jasper, 4 navy, 6 bronze, 10 jasper, 4 navy.

Table loom: use 2 dents per cm in your reed, i.e. one slot and one hole, miss one slot and one hole, thread one slot and one hole, etc.

Four-shaft loom: use reed with 2 dents per cm and serge pattern:

```
        4   4   4
      3   3   3
    2   2   2
  1   1   1     etc.
```

WEAVING: Use plain weave and only the jasper mohair.

Fronts: start by weaving the fronts side by side, each 40 cm wide (80 threads) for a length of 85 cm. Then leave 10 threads at either side for the sleeve openings and weave a further 7 cm.
Leave 20 cm unwoven warp.

Back: Cut off 18 threads on either side so that you are weaving over a width of 62 cm. Weave 85 cm in length, leave 10 threads on either side and continue for a further 7 cm.
Leave 20 cm warp unwoven.

Yokes

Fronts: cut off 6 warp threads on either side. Divide the 112 remaining threads into two (56 threads) which you weave with 2 separate shuttles.
When the work measures 10 cm begin decreasing for the neck on either side of the front opening, decreasing every 2 picks: 14 threads, 5 threads, 5 threads, 2 threads, 2 threads, 2 threads. Continue straight until the work measures 24 cm.
Leave 20 cm unwoven warp.

Sleeves: cut off 6 warp threads on either side, so that your weaving is now 50 cm wide. Weave a length of 60 cm for the first sleeve.
Leave 20 cm unwoven warp.
Weave a second sleeve identical to the first.
Leave 20 cm unwoven warp.

Yokes (contd.)

Back: cut off 8 warp threads on either side so that your weaving is 42 cm wide. Weave a length of 18 cm.
Your weaving is now finished, remove from the loom.

FINISHING: Cut your sections through the middle of the unwoven warp. Press with a damp cloth or steam iron.
For finishing off the warp threads, see 'Finishing'.
Gather the top of the back and sew to the yoke. Gather the fronts and sew to the two front yokes.
Sew the back and fronts together at the shoulders (with a slightly diagonal row of stitching) and sides.
Sew up the sleeves with either a straight row of stitching or a diagonal one if you want the sleeves to taper to the cuffs.
Sew the sleeves into the arm holes.
Fold 5 cm back at each front edge for

the facings. Hem the bottom of the coat and sleeves. Make fastenings either with buttons or press-studs.

SCARF: Make a second warp of 40 threads (20 cm wide) and 2.40 m long. Weave the scarf in plain weave using oddments of wool left over from weaving the coat. Since these threads will be in various colours make the warp entirely in jasper wool.

When the work measures 1.80 m remove from loom, press and tie into fringes. (See pattern on previous page.)

Child's Jacket (Any size)

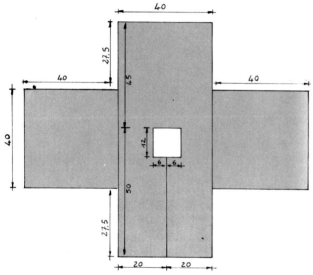

Before starting see:
Finishing Stitch - Unspun Wool - Finishing

MATERIALS: about 100 g country-style wool, about 300 g graduated unspun wool

HOW TO WORK OUT YOUR PATTERN: The size given in our example is for age 8. It is quite simple to make it fit your child in the following way:

Take his hip measurement (stomach measurement for small children), total length of the jacket, arm length (measure with the arm slightly bent), length of sleeve opening (this will vary depending upon whether the jacket will be worn indoors or out of doors over sweaters).

Divide the hip measurement by 2 and add 4 cm seam allowance.
    e.g 72 cm ÷ 2 = 36 + 4 = 40 cm.
    This 40 cm is the width of the body of the jacket.

Multiply the length of the sleeve opening by 2.
    e.g. 20 cm × 2 = 40 cm.
    This gives the width of the sleeve.

To determine the number of threads you need, you multiply the larger of these two measurements by 2 (generally it will be the body measurement). In our example the body and sleeve widths are identical.
    e.g. 40 × 2 = 80 threads.

To calculate the length of the body, measure the child to find the length of the back, and add the same length again for the fronts + 5 cm for the shoulder.
    e.g. 45 + 45 + 5 = 95 cm.

To calculate the total length of thread necessary to make your jacket add the total length of the jacket to 20 cm unwoven warp to allow for cutting, the length of your first sleeve, another 20 cm unwoven warp, the length of the second sleeve and the total allowance for attaching to the loom (60 cm).
    e.g. 95 + 20 + 40 + 20 + 40 + 60 = 2.75 m.

WARP: For our example make a warp of 80 threads, 2.75 m in length.

Table loom: thread your reed in an unusual way: thread 1 hole, miss 1 slot, thread 1 hole, miss 1 slot and 1 hole, thread 1 slot, miss 1 hole, thread 1 slot, miss 1 hole and 1 slot, thread 1 hole, miss 1 slot, thread 1 hole, miss 1 slot and 1 hole, etc.

Four-shaft loom: use reed with 2 dents per cm and serge pattern:

```
        4    4    4
      3    3    3
    2    2    2 ,
  1    1    1      etc.
```
The order of shafts will be: 1–4
                             2–3

The body: Use your warp thread to begin with a row of finishing stitch, then weave the 45 cm for the back in unspun wool (see 'Unspun wool'). Then work the square neck by leaving 24 threads unwoven at the centre of the warp. Weave only the threads for the shoulders on either side of the neck opening, i.e. your warp width *minus* 24 threads ÷ 2.
    e.g. 80 threads – 24 threads = 56

threads ÷ 2 = 28 threads for each shoulder.

Weave a further 12 cm and then pick up 12 threads on the left and 12 on the right.

e.g. Weave on 40 threads on the left-hand side and 40 on the right, leaving a slit down the centre to separate the fronts.

Measure the length of the back + 5 cm from the start of the neck.

e.g. 50 cm.

You have now finished the body of the jacket, finish each front with finishing stitch.

Leave 20 cm unwoven warp.

The sleeves: If necessary reduce the width of your warp, depending on your sleeve width.

Weave the length given by measuring the arm.

e.g. 40 cm wide gives 80 threads and a length of 40 cm.

Leave 20 cm unwoven warp.

Weave a second length identical to the first sleeve.

FINISHING: Remove your weaving from loom, press with a damp cloth or steam iron and see 'Finishing' for how to finish the warp threads. Position your sleeves as shown in the diagram and sew in.

Fold the jacket to the wrong side and sew the underside of the sleeves and sides of the jacket with a continuous line of stitching.

Small animal-shaped buttons have been sewn on to decorate the body of the jacket and the sleeves.

Striped Skirt with Flat Pleats (Any size)

Before starting see:
Finishing Stitch - Finishing

MATERIALS: 1 kg country-style wool in several colours, sewing machine

WARP: Make a warp of 320 threads alternating the different coloured wools in any way you wish.

Table loom: Your warp should be 2.40 m in length. Use every dent in the reed.

Four-shaft loom: Your warp will be 2.60 m in length. Thread the heddles for serge pattern:

```
    4   4   4
   3   3   3
  2   2   2
 1   1   1    etc.
```

WEAVING: Weave 2 m in plain weave in one colour only.

FINISHING: It is essential to use a sewing machine.

Measure your waist, add 4 cm for seams and 80 cm for the flat pleats.

e.g. for a waist measurement of 66 cm, you get 66 + 4 + 80 = 1.50 m.

Fold the length of weaving in half to give a length of weaving 1 m in length by 80 cm wide. Divide the waist + seams + pleats measurement by two (e.g.: 75 cm).

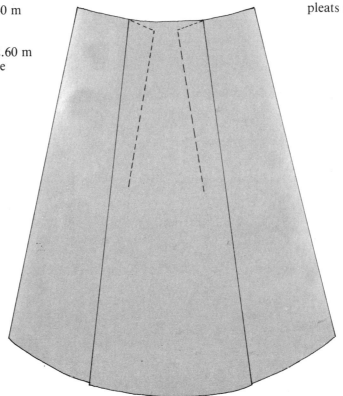

Centre this measurement on your weaving, placing a small pin at either side to mark the length (e.g. 17.5 cm, pin, 75 cm, pin, 17.5 cm).

Use a ruler to find the diagonal from each pin to the opposite edge of the skirt (see sketch), and tack along this line on both back and front (4 lines of tacking). Sew along these lines with either a very short zig-zag stitch, or three rows of straight stitch. Cut the 2 panels 1 cm beyond the stitching.

Sew together along one side, leaving a 12 cm opening on the other.

Lay the skirt flat on the right side with the side seams one upon the other. Place a pin on the right and one on the left 20 cm from the edge (see sketch).

Unfold your skirt and rearrange with the side seams opposite, flatten out the two tucks made by the pins to make the flat pleats. Tack round the waist and sew into a waist band 12 cm wide and folded in two. You can make this waistband from the lengths of weaving cut off at either edge. Use several pieces oversewn around each edge with a very small zig-zag stitch or 3 lines of straight stitch.

Sew a 12 cm zip into the opening you have left and sew a button to the waistband. Make a loop from one of your coloured wools.

Try the skirt on and make a hem.

If lined the skirt will keep its shape better.

Long Dress in Pink Mohair (One size, to fit 81.5 cm to 91.5 cm bust)

Before starting see:
Finishing Stitch - Mohair Wool -
Finishing

MATERIALS: 250 g pink mohair wool—
50 g white, 100 g pink lamé

WARP: Make a warp of 180 threads
alternating 20 threads pink mohair, 20
threads pink mohair and lamé together, 40
threads pink mohair only, 20 threads pink
mohair and lamé together, 40 threads pink
mohair only, 20 threads mohair and lamé
together, 20 threads mohair only. The
warp should be 4 m in length.

Table loom: thread your reed with 1 slot
and 1 hole, miss 1 slot and 1 hole, thread 1
slot and 1 hole, miss 1 slot and 1 hole, etc.

Four-shaft loom: Use reed with 2 dents per
cm and thread heddles for serge pattern:

```
        4   4   4
      3   3   3
    2   2   2
  1   1   1     etc.
```

WEAVING: Do not put too much wool on
your shuttle so that you can alternate picks
of mohair alone and picks of mohair with
lame in rapid succession.

To shape the sides of your dress decrease
1 thread at the start of the pick on the
right and 1 thread at the end of the pick
on the left every 3 cm.

When the work measures 1.25 m you
should have decreased 40 threads on either
side, giving a width of 100 threads (i.e.
width of 50 cm).

Now pick up all the warp threads to
make the sleeves and work a further
25 cm.

Now fill a second shuttle with pink
mohair (or mohair and lamé, depending on
the stage of the pattern reached) to weave
the shoulders on either side of the neck
opening.

With your right-hand shuttle weave the
70 right-hand threads, and with the left-
hand shuttle weave the 70 threads on the
left. The 40 threads remaining at the centre
are not woven.

Weave a length of 8 cm with the 2
shuttles, then gradually pick up the neck
opening threads, increasing with both
shuttles: 2 threads to start with, 4 threads
the second time, 4 threads again the 3rd
time, 6 threads the 4th time. Then use 1
shuttle to weave the whole width.

When you have woven 50 cm beyond the
sleeve increase, decrease 40 threads on the
right-hand side and then 40 on the left so
that you are once more weaving on a width
of 50 cm for the bust.

Then increase one thread at either side
every 3 cm until 1.25 m later you are again
weaving the whole warp.

Leave 20 cm warp unwoven.

Cut off 20 threads on either side of the
warp. This leaves 140 threads (i.e. 70 cm)
on which you weave a length of 35 cm for
the roll collar.

The collar is woven in white mohair and
lamé together.

FINISHING: Remove weaving from
loom, press with damp cloth or steam iron,
separate collar from dress through the
centre of the unwoven warp.

Fold the dress in two across the centre of
the sleeve. Sew the underside of the sleeves
and sides together with a continuous row
of stitching.

Turn to the right side, sew the two ends
of the collar together and then sew it
around the neck opening, gathering it
slightly, and fold it over 3 times.

Try on the dress and make the hem.

To improve the finishing of the dress
you can crochet a narrow length in lamé
around the sleeve and neck edges (once
folded).

Press the seams with an iron.

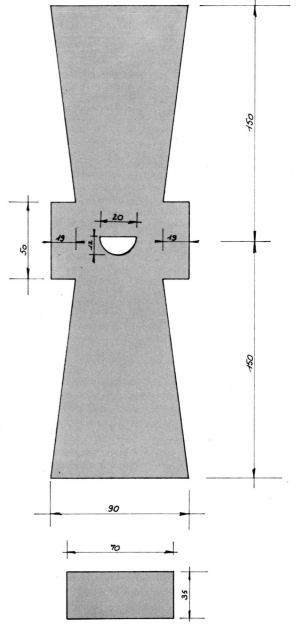

Andes Cape

Before starting see:
Finishing Stitch - Finishing

MATERIALS: 250 g cashmere wool for the warp, 700 g camel hair wool for the weft, sewing machine.

WARP: This cape is made from 4 panels 60 cm × 60 cm, joined into a square, so it can be made on a small loom. Make a warp of 120 threads, 3.60 m in length.

Table loom: The stitch used in the pattern is serge, but there is no reason why you can't make it in plain weave, the only stitch you can use with this loom. Thread your reed with 2 dents per cm, i.e. thread 1 slot and 1 hole, miss 1 slot and 1 hole, thread 1 slot and 1 hole, etc.

Four-shaft loom: use reed with 2 dents per cm and serge pattern:

```
        4   4   4
      3   3   3
    2   2   2
  1   1   1    etc.
```

WEFT

Table loom: Weave 4 identical squares 60 × 60 cm, separated by 20 cm unwoven warp so that you can cut between them eventually.

Four-shaft loom: The stitch used is serge.
Begin with 1 pick plain weave so that you can do your finishing stitch, then weave 60 cm repeating the following pedal combinations:

```
      1—4
      1—2
      2—3
      3—4
```

Finish with a pick of plain weave for the finishing stitch.
Leave a band of unwoven warp.
Make the 3 other sections in the same way, separating each with 20 cm unwoven warp.

FINISHING: When you have completed the 4 sections, remove work from loom, press with steam iron or damp cloth, separate the sections by cutting through the centre of the unwoven warp and turn to 'Finishing' for how to finish off the warp threads.
Join the sections together as in the diagram to form one large square, 1.20 m × 1.20 m.
Lay this square out flat. At the top left-hand corner (see diagram) place a pin 30 cm on either side of the corner. Again with a pin attach a thread from the centre point to the left-hand pin at the edge. Cut your thread to this length. Turn the thread about its axis between the 2 pins placed 30 cm from the corner. With a pin mark the length at 6 separate points. Then tack from one pin to the next. This gives the rounded edge of the neck.
Measure 20 cm to the left of the top right-hand corner and 20 cm to the right of the bottom left-hand corner. Attach another thread from the centre point to one of these pins, cut off the thread to this length and pivot it about its axis from the pin on the bottom left-hand edge to the pin near the top right-hand corner. Mark 12 separate points and tack.
Sew along the tacking with a double zig-zag or triple straight stitch row and cut around the edges.

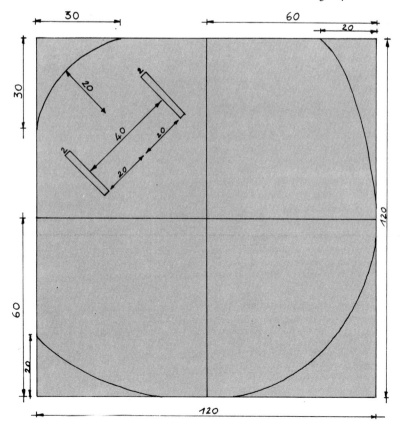

Tack a slanting line along the diagonal formed in this way. Measure 20 cm from the shorter round edge, mark with a pin and measure 20 cm again from this pin and mark again with a pin. Measure 20 cm from the first pin on either side of the diagonal and 20 cm from the second pin. Tack parallel with these two last pins to mark the arm holes (see diagram).

Sew with double zig-zag or triple straight stitch with the machine 1 cm either side of the tacking thread to give a rectangle 2 cm × 20 cm. Cut a slit between the two 20 cm lines of stitching.

Braid all your seams, the edges of the arm holes, and with a crochet hook make fringes all round the cape (see 'Fringes').

Mohair Jacket with Motif (One size, to fit 81.5 cm to 91.5 cm bust)

Before starting see:
Finishing Stitch - Mohair Wool -
Finishing

MATERIALS

Warp: 200 g ecru cotton

Weft: 300 g ecru mohair

Motifs: 50 g coloured wool: 3 lengths

WARP: Make a warp of 260 threads, 2.10 m in length.

Table loom: use all the dents in your reed (65 cm × 4 threads).

Four-shaft loom: use no. 4 reed (4 dents per cm).
   The heddles are threaded for serge pattern:

```
      4   4   4
    3   3   3
  2   2   2
1   1   1    etc.
```

WEAVING: Stitch used is plain weave.
   The article is made in one piece. Start with the sides and load 2 shuttles with ecru mohair wool.
   Divide the warp into two: do a row of finishing stitch with the end of your right-hand shuttle for the 130 right-hand threads, and one with the end of your left-hand shuttle for the 130 left-hand threads. Thread your 2 shuttles into the same pick

simultaneously so that decreases on either side will coincide.
   To shape the sides of your jacket, decrease 1 thread on either side every 1.5 cm until the width is 50 cm (i.e. decrease 28 times on either side, making a length of 42 to 45 cm).

The motif: When the work measures 25 cm begin your motif on the right front. The birds claw begins at the 29th thread from the inside edge. Based on this follow the diagram given, which should be interpreted as follows.

Table loom: thread a needle with a long length of coloured wool (double if the wool is fine). Don't worry about the figures in the right-hand margin; the figures at the top show the number of threads in the motif, the numbers in the left-hand margin show the number of picks in the motif.

   Have your warp threads as flat as possible (the smallest shed possible) and interpret the motif in this way: the uncoloured squares represent the over threads, the coloured squares represent the threads covered with your needle.

1st pick: go over the 29th and 30th threads, starting from the inside edge, go under the next 6 threads, over 2 more warp threads, under the next 6, over the following 2, under 6, over 2.
   Leave your needle ready under the weaving and work one pick of ordinary plain weave with your shuttle of mohair wool.

2nd pick: make the shed flat again, take your needle and cover the same threads as on the previous row. Leave your needle ready under the weaving and weave 1 pick plain weave with your shuttle of mohair.

3rd pick: go over the 31st and 32nd threads, under 2 warp threads, over 2 threads, under 8 warp threads, over 2 threads, under 2 threads, and over 2 threads again, leaving your needle ready under the weaving. Weave 1 pick plain weave with the shuttle.

4th pick: go over the 2 threads which you went under on the previous pick, between the spurs, go under 14 warp threads and over the following 2. Leave the needle ready underneath and weave 1 pick plain weave with the shuttle.

5th and 6th rows are identical to the 4th. Remember to weave 1 pick with the shuttle in plain weave between each row of the motif.

7th row: go over the 27th and 28th threads, under 2 threads, over the next 2, under 2 threads, over 2, under 2, over 2, under 2, over 2, under 2, over 2, under 2, over 2, under 2, over 2, under 2, over 2. Leave your needle ready underneath, and weave 1 pick plain weave with the shuttle.
   Now that you understand the principle you can follow the pattern.

Four-shaft loom: the top line of numbers shows the number of threads of the motif. The numbers in the left-hand margin show the number of rows. The numbers in the right-hand margin show the pedal combinations which give a corrugated pattern (plain weave 2/2).

1st row: open your shed with 1/4 and insert a needle of coloured thread (used double if the wool is fine) from underneath between the 28th and 29th threads. The 29th thread should be among the layer of threads resting on the leaf of the reed—lower layer of threads—(however, depending on whether the loom is raised or lowered, your 29th thread may not be in the lower layer of threads, in which case it is easier to bring out the needle between the 30th and 31st threads and to change the top line of numbers). Once your needle is in position, go over the 29th and 30th threads (or 31st and 32nd), leave 2 top threads, 2 bottom threads, 2 top threads, taking your needle underneath the weaving; go over the next 2 bottom threads, under 2 top threads, 2 bottom threads, 2 top threads; over the next 2 top threads, under 2 top threads, 2 bottom threads, 2 top threads; over the next 2 bottom threads; under 2 top threads, 2 bottom threads, 2 top threads, over the next 2 bottom threads. Leave your needle ready underneath and weave 1 pick plain weave with your shuttle of mohair (1/3 or 3/4, this shed should be opposite to the preceding one).

2nd row: again lower shafts 1 and 4 (number given in right-hand margin) and work with your needle in the same way as in the preceding row. Weave one pick plain weave with the shuttle.

3rd row: lower shafts 2 and 3, bring out your needle between threads 28 and 29 (30 and 31), go over the 29th and 30th threads (31 and 32), leave 2 top threads, go over the next 2 bottom threads, leave 2 top threads, 2 bottom threads, 2 top threads, 2 bottom threads, 2 top threads; go over the next 2 bottom threads, leave the 2 top threads and go over the next 2 bottom threads. Leave your needle ready on the wrong side and weave 1 pick plain weave with your shuttle.

4th row: go back to 1/4 and go over the 2 threads which you went under on the previous row. These 2 threads represent the claw of the bird between the spurs. Leave the next 2 top threads, then the bottom 2, the top 2, the bottom 2, the top 2, the bottom 2, the top 2, go over the next 2 threads for the second claw.

Leave your needle ready. Weave your plain weave pick.

5th and 6th rows are identical to the 4th, remembering to alternate your picks of plain weave.

7th row: set shafts 2 and 3, bring out your needle between the 25th and 26th threads and go over the whole of the lower layer of threads as far as the 60th thread. Leave your needle ready and weave 1 pick plain weave.

8th row: identical to the 7th, weave 1 pick plain weave between the two.

9th row: bring out the needle (still with shafts 2 and 3) between the 21st and 22nd threads, go over all the lower layer of threads to the 64th thread. Leave your needle ready and weave 1 pick plain weave.

You should now understand the procedure and be able to follow the pattern.

REMARKS: The motif will determine the right and wrong side of the work. Leave most of your ends of thread on the wrong side, you will sew them into the motif with a needle when you have finished.

Don't forget—when weaving your picks of plain mohair—to weave both fronts together (so that the decreases are even). So you also have to weave a pick of plain weave on the left front. Doing the pattern should not make you forget your decreases.

When the work measures 45 cm, soon after the motif, increase for the sleeve. Your shuttles on each front have to pick up the whole width of the warp, i.e. 130 threads on each side. Weave a further 12 cm in this way, then decrease at the centre on each pick (for the neck) as follows:

Decrease 10 threads, then 8, then 6, then 4, so that you have decreased 28 threads on each front. Measuring from the first decrease of 10 threads weave the remaining 102 threads for a further 14 cm.

Then use 1 shuttle only to weave right across the warp for a length of 25 cm.

Then leave the 28 threads on the right which form the right sleeve, and when the shuttle returns to the left-hand side, leave the 28 threads of the left sleeve.

Then increase in the same way that you decreased on the fronts, i.e. 1 thread every 1.5 cm so that at the end of the work you have picked up your 28 threads.

Finish off the sleeves and neck with finishing stitch.

When the work measures 50 cm from the sleeve decrease, and you have picked up all your warp threads, do another row of finishing stitch to finish off the jacket.

FINISHING: Remove weaving from loom, press with a damp cloth or steam iron. Cut through the middle of your decreased threads, but leave the 3 decreased threads near the sleeves, which will not interfere with your sewing and could fray if cut.

Fold the weaving over at the centre of the sleeves, and sew up the side seams. The underside of the sleeves are not sewn.

Oversew all edges. If you have no sewing machine, or for more detailed instructions, turn to 'Finishing'.

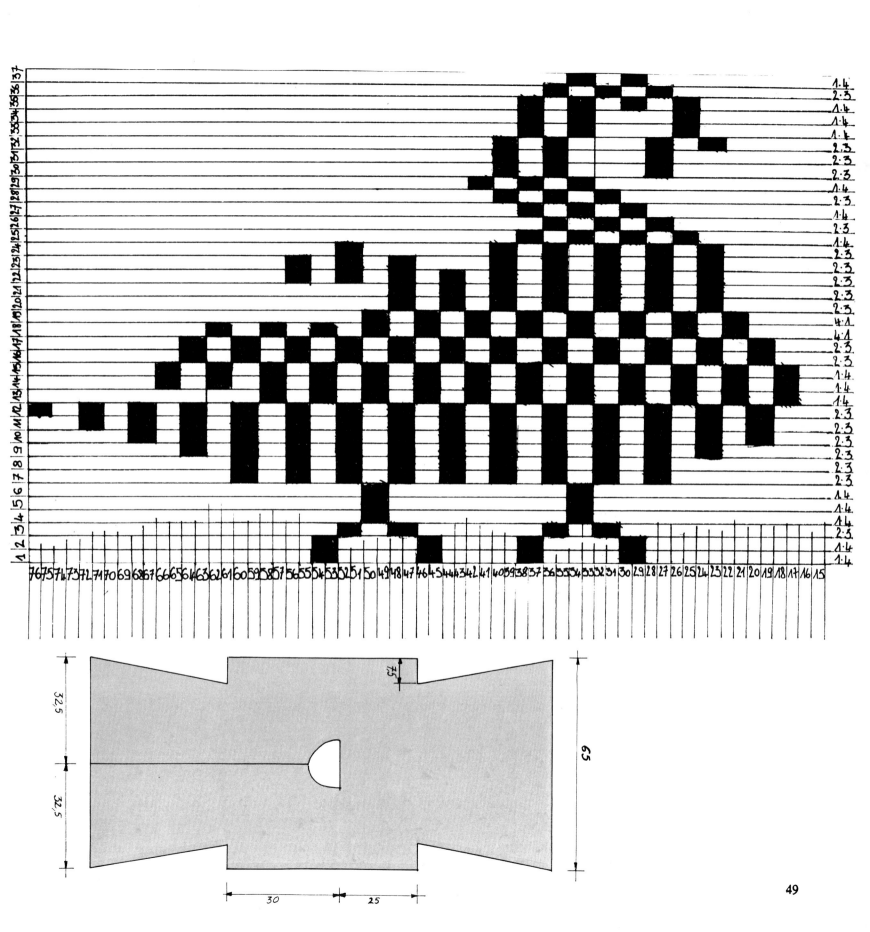

49

Mohair Bolero (To fit bust sizes 76 cm, 81.5 cm, 86.5 cm and 91.5 cm)

Before starting see:
Finishing Stitch - Unspun Wool -
Mohair Wool - Finishing

MATERIALS: 150 g mohair wool (120 g light pink—15 g violet—15 g fuchsia), 50 g unspun wool.

WARP: Make a warp of 92 (94 – 96 – 98) threads, with alternate bands of mohair of any colour or width you wish.
 The length of the warp is 1.70 m.

Table loom: thread your reed with 1 slot and 1 hole, miss 1 slot and 1 hole, thread 1 slot and 1 hole, etc.

Four-shaft loom: Use no. 2 reed and thread heddles for serge pattern:

```
    4   4   4
   3   3   3
  2   2   2
 1   1   1      etc.
```

WEAVING: Work entirely in pink mohair using the whole width of the warp until the work measures 25 cm, then decrease for the sleeves, 10 threads on either side.
 Continue weaving on these 72 (74 – 76 – 78) threads for a further 24 cm.
 Then take 2 shuttles of pink wool. Leave the decreased sleeve threads and weave 28 threads with the right-hand shuttle, leave 16 unwoven threads, and with the left-hand shuttle weave the remaining 28 threads on the left, for a further 10 cm.

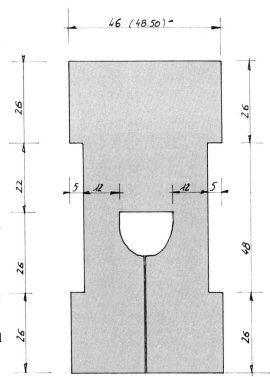

Size 76 cm bust: gradually pick up with each shuttle the 16 neck threads, increasing 3 times: 2 threads the first time, 2 threads for the second and 4 threads for the 3rd increase.

For size 81.5 cm bust: weave 28 threads on each shoulder, leaving 18 threads for the neck which are picked up in 3 stages: 2 threads—3 threads—4 threads.

For size 86.5 cm bust: weave 28 threads on each shoulder. The 20 neck threads are picked up in 3 stages: 2 threads—4 threads—4 threads.

For size 91.5 cm bust: weave 30 threads for each shoulder. The 18 neck threads are picked up in 3 stages: 2 threads—3 threads—4 threads.
 Your shuttles should now be at the centre. Continue weaving with two shuttles to make the front opening. When you have woven a further 14 cm, pick up the 10 right-hand sleeve threads with your right shuttle, and the 10 left-hand sleeve threads with the left shuttle.
 Weave a further 25 cm.

UNSPUN WOOL: Intersperse bands of unspun wool in the fronts as you wish (see 'Unspun Wool').

FINISHING: Remove weaving from loom, press with damp cloth or steam iron.
 See 'Finishing' for how to finish off the threads.
 Fold the body of the bolero into two and sew up the sides.

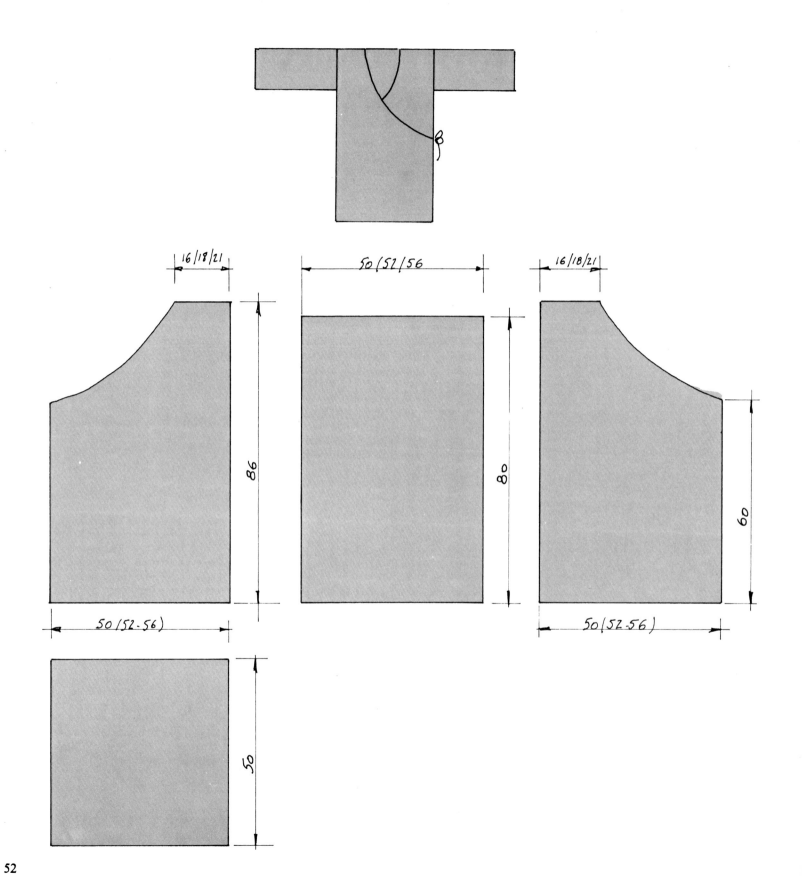

16/18/21

50 (52/56

16/18/21

86

80

50 (52-56)

60

50 (52-56)

50

Chinese Jacket (Sizes to fit 86.5 cm to 96.5 cm bust)

Before starting see:
Finishing Stitch - Fabric Weaving -
Finishing

MATERIALS

Warp: 250 g ecru cotton

Weft: strips of fabric

WARP: Make a warp of 100 (104 – 112) threads, 4.20 m in length.

Table loom: use 2 threads per cm, i.e. thread 1 slot and 1 hole, miss 1 slot and 1 hole, thread 1 slot and 1 hole, etc.

Four-shaft loom: use no. 2 reed and thread heddles for serge pattern:

```
        4   4   4
      3   3   3
    2   2   2
  1   1   1    etc.
```

WEAVING

Back: Using the whole width of the warp weave a length of 80 cm. Leave 20 cm unwoven warp.

Fronts: Again using the whole width of the warp, weave a length of 60 cm, then begin decreasing for the neck.

Decrease gradually on the left-hand side as follows: 20 threads—then 16—then 12—then 8—then 4, and 4 again. You have now dropped 68 threads, leaving 16 (18 – 21) cm for shoulders.

Continue weaving on these threads until the work measures 26 cm from your first decrease (the 20 thread decrease).

The first front is finished, leave 20 cm unwoven warp, and weave a second front identical to the first. When you have finished the second front, leave another 20 cm unwoven warp.

Sleeves: For size 86.5 cm bust keep all the warp threads, for sizes 91.5 cm and 96.5 cm bust reduce the width by 4 and 12 threads respectively, to give a width of 50 cm.

Weave a length of 50 cm, leave 20 cm unwoven warp and make a second sleeve, also 50 cm in length.

FINISHING: Remove weaving from loom, press with damp cloth or steam iron, separate sections by cutting through centre of unwoven warp.

For how to finish off the threads, turn to 'Finishing'.

Sew the two front shoulders to the back, lay flat and sew in the sleeves, with the centre of the sleeve to the shoulder seam.

Sew the undersides of the sleeves and sides of the jacket together.

Sew two lengths of cotton bias binding in colours to match your fabric all around the neck, leaving 20 cm at either end to serve as ties. For the ties under the arms, sew two 20 cm lengths of binding under each sleeve, attached to the binding around the neck.

Woven-Fabric Screen

Before starting see:
Finishing Stitch - Fabric Weaving -
Finishing

MATERIALS: White-wood screen, stained walnut.

Warp: 300 g cotton.

Weft: strips of fabric in several colours.

WARP: Make a warp to fit the size of the open screen panels.

Our screen has 4 panels, 35 cm wide × 60 cm long and 4 panels 35 cm wide × 40 cm high.

The weaving for these panels should measure 37 × 65 cm and 37 × 45 cm, so that the edges can be turned under before fixing to the screen.

So we make a warp of 74 threads (37 cm × 2 threads per cm = 74 threads). The length will be: 65 (1st top panel) + 20 (unwoven warp) + 65 + 20 + 65 + 20 + 65 + 20 + 45 (1st bottom panel) + 20 + 45 + 20 + 45 + 20 + 45 + 60 (total warp lost for attaching to loom) = 6.40 m.

Table loom: thread 1 slot and 1 hole, miss 1 slot and 1 hole, thread 1 slot and 1 hole, etc, in your reed.

Four-shaft loom: use no. 2 reed and thread for serge pattern:

```
    4   4   4
  3   3   3
2   2   2
1   1   1      etc.
```

WEAVING: For the first panel weave 2 cm using the warp cotton, then 60 cm with fabric, finishing with 2 cm in warp cotton.

Leave 20 cm unwoven warp, weave a second identical panel, leave another 20 cm, weave the 3rd panel, leave 20 cm unwoven warp and weave the 4th panel.

When you have woven these 4 top panels, weave the 4 bottom panels, leaving 20 cm unwoven warp between each section.

Use the colours of your fabric to create a different look for each panel.

FINISHING: Remove weaving from loom, separate panels by cutting through the centre of the unwoven warp, press sections with damp cloth or steam iron. Turn to 'Finishing' for how to finish off threads.

Using a stapler or small upholstery tacks, fix your panels to the screen, folding in the bands of cotton (between the weaving and the screen).

Decorative Panel

Before starting see:
Finishing Stitch - Unspun Wool -
Raw Wool - Finishing

MATERIALS: about 250 g oddments of green wool in different shades, about 200 g oddments of pink wool in different shades, 50 g fine bouclé wool in dark violet.

Wool fleece: 20 g blue, pink, green, ecru, 150 g warp cotton

WARP: Make a warp of 200 threads, 1.50 m in length.

Table loom: use 2 dents per cm in your reed; thread 1 slot and 1 hole, miss 1 slot and 1 hole, thread 1 slot and 1 hole, etc.

Four-shaft loom: Use reed with 2 dents per cm and serge pattern:

```
    4   4   4
   3   3   3
  2   2   2
 1   1   1    etc.
```

WEAVING: Stitch used is plain weave.

Begin with a row of finishing stitch then work irregular areas with your green wools until you have woven half the panel, working as follows. Work in 2 colours for each pick, introducing them from opposite ends on the first pick, and bringing them out between the same 2 threads on the next pick. If you then take each shuttle back to the side you will have 1 thread which has not been woven and a slit between the two colours.

To avoid this, cross one shuttle over the other so that the threads cross. Work the thread that would otherwise be left with the shuttle which you wrapped round the other colour.

You can have more colours in the same pick so long as you always keep 2 shuttles opposite one another, then the second shuttle end to end with the 3rd, the 4th facing the 3rd, etc.

To vary the texture add tufts of fleece into some picks of plain weave.

When the work measures 45 cm start your open circle. Draw a circle onto cardboard (around a plate, for example), cut it out, place on your warp and draw the shape onto your tensioned threads with a black felt-tip pen.

Weave around this circle working a few picks of green wool on the inside to give an irregular shape.

When you are about 20 picks from the base of the circle, introduce some pink and a little of the bouclé to form a transition from green to pink.

Work 4 picks beyond the circle and finish off the unwoven threads. Thread a needle with your pink wool to oversew the threads (taking two at a time). Leave some free.

Continue weaving normally and include a few tufts of pink/blue and ecru fleece in the last quarter of the panel.

Your panel should be 90 cm long.

Cut off your weaving. Tie the top fringes to a thick wooden pole. Knot the bottom threads in 2 rows of alternating knots.

Sew a length of weighted cotton tape to the bottom of your panel to weight it.

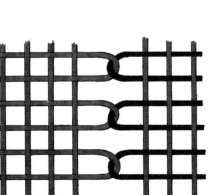

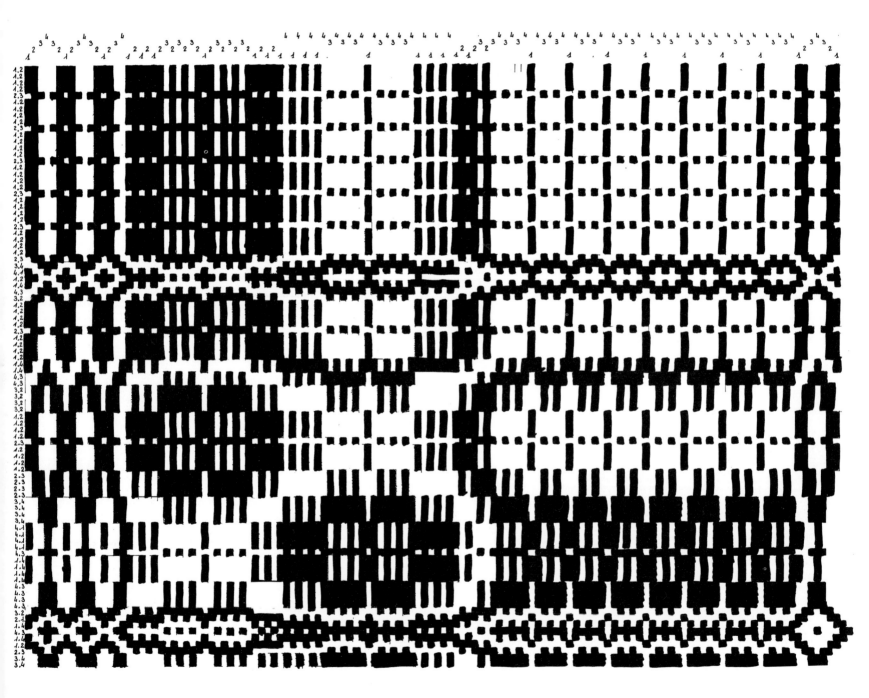

Before starting see:
Finishing Stitch - Finishing

Ecru Pouffe

MATERIALS: 400 g warp cotton, 200 g unspun cotton

WARP: This pattern can only be made on a four-shaft loom. Make a warp of 247 threads, 3.20 m in length.

Use a reed with 4 dents per cm and thread the heddles as follows:

```
 4   4   4                4 4 4 4 4 4 4 4 4 4 4 4         4
  3 3   3 3   3       3 3 3   3 3 3            3 3 3   3 3 3        3 3
 2   2 2   2 2    2 2 2 2 2 2 2 2 2 2 2                      2 2 2
 1   1   1   1 1 1        1           1 1 1 1 1 1        1         1 1 1 1 1

 4 4 4 4 4 4 4 4 4       4 4 4 4 4 4 4 4 4 4 4 4 4
  3 3   3 3   3 3   3 3           3 3 3   3 3 3            3 3 3   3 3 3
               2 2 2                2 2 2 2 2 2 2 2 2 2 2 2
    1     1     1    1 1 1 1 1        1        1 1 1 1 1 1   1         1 1 1

 4     4     4
  3   3 3   3 3
   2 2   2 2   2
    1     1     1
```

WEAVING: Fill 2 shuttles; one with warp cotton—one with unspun cotton.

Begin with 1 pick plain weave for your finishing stitch, then use the following pedal combinations, alternating 1 pick warp cotton (c) with 1 pick unspun cotton (m).

1-2 m	1-2 m	1-2 m	3-4 m	2-3 m	2-3 m	2-3 m	4-1 m	3-2 m
1-3 c	1-3 c	1-3 c	1-3 c	1-3 c	1-3 c	1-3 c	1-3 c	1-3 c
1-2 m	1-2 m	1-2 m	4-1 m	1-2 m	2-3 m	2-3 m	4-3 m	2-1 m
2-4 c	2-4 c	2-4 c	2-4 c	2-4 c	2-4 c	2-4 c	2-4 c	2-4 c
1-2 m	1-2 m	1-2 m	1-2 m	1-2 m	2-3 m	2-3 m	1-4 m	1-4 m
1-3 c	1-3 c	1-3 c	1-3 c	1-3 c	1-3 c	1-3 c	1-3 c	1-3 c
1-2 m	1-2 m	1-2 m	1-4 m	1-2 m	1-2 m	3-4 m	1-4 m	4-3 m
2-4 c	2-4 c	2-4 c	2-4 c	2-4 c	2-4 c	2-4 c	2-4 c	2-4 c
2-3 m	2-3 m	2-3 m	4-3 m	1-2 m	1-2 m	3-4 m	1-4 m	
1-3 c	1-3 c	1-3 c	1-3 c	1-3 c	1-3 c	1-3 c	1-3 c	
1-2 m	1-2 m	1-2 m	3-2 m	1-4 m	1-2 m	3-4 m	1-4 m	
2-4 c	2-4 c	2-4 c	2-4 c	2-4 c	2-4 c	2-4 c	2-4 c	
1-2 m	1-2 m	1-2 m	1-2 m	1-4 m	1-2 m	3-4 m	4-3 m	
1-3 c	1-3 c	1-3 c	1-3 c	1-3 c	1-3 c	1-3 c	1-3 c	
1-2 m	1-2 m	1-2 m	1-2 m	4-3 m	3-2 m	4-1 m	4-3 m	
2-4 c	2-4 c	2-4 c	2-4 c	2-4 c	2-4 c	2-4 c	2-4 c	
1-2 m	1-2 m	1-2 m	1-2 m	4-3 m	1-2 m	4-1 m	4-3 m	
1-3 c	1-3 c	1-3 c	1-3 c	1-3 c	1-3 c	1-3 c	1-3c	
2-3 m	2-3 m	2-3 m	1-2 m	3-2 m	1-2 m	4-1 m	4-3 m	
2-4 c	2-4 c	2-4 c	2-4 c	2-4 c	2-4 c	2-4 c	2-4 c	

When you have come to the end of these combinations work through them again in reverse order: 4-3, 1-3, 1-4, 2-4, 2-1, 1-3, 3-2, 2-4, etc.

Finish with a row of finishing stitch in warp cotton.

Leave 20 cm unwoven warp.

Weave a length of 2.50 m to go around the pouffe.

FINISHING: Remove weaving from loom, press with steam iron or damp cloth.

Cut threads between sections and turn to 'Finishing' for how to finish off threads.

Make a cushion for your pouffe from cotton, cutting out 2 squares 62 cm by 62 cm and a length of 40 cm by 2.50 m. Wrap this long band around the first square, tack and sew over the tacking. Repeat for the second square, placing it exactly opposite the first.

Stuff the cushion through the open seam at the end of the long strip. When it is well stuffed sew up the seam by hand.

In the same way sew the length of weaving around the top and also sew the two ends of the strip together.

Make a hem 4 cm wide at the bottom of the strip, and with a darning needle thread a strong cord through it.

Cover the cushion with the weaving.

Draw up the string so that the cover encloses the pouffe.

Double-Weave Bedspread (2.40 m × 2.50 m)

MATERIALS

Warp: 300 g coloured cottons.

Weft: Strips of old fabric, cut along the whole length to a width of about 2 cm.

200 g raw wool, 200 g unspun wool, oddments of ordinary wool in colours to match the fabric strips.

WARP: This bedspread is made on a loom with a 1.20 m reed.

The reed used is a no. 4 reed.

The double weave can only be done on a four-shaft loom.

Make a warp of 480 threads, alternating your cottons in any way you wish, 3.20 m in length.

The heddles are threaded with the traditional pattern:

```
      4   4
    3   3
  2   2
1   1    etc.
```

WEAVING: The following combinations are repeated:

```
        1
        3
        134
        123
```

This will give one layer of weaving on the uneven shafts, and one on the even shafts. These two layers lie one upon the other, closed at one end and open at the other edge.

To obtain a length of weaving that can be opened out, pass your weft through the sheds without trying to pick up the edges (this would give a tubular length of weaving).

Mix colours and materials in any way you wish.

FINISHING: When you have woven 2.70 m (20 cm shrinkage allowance), cut off the weaving and finish it at once knotting 6 to 8 threads together to make fringes. Since the weaving consists of two layers one upon the other it is impossible to begin and end with finishing stitch.

Open out your weaving and press out the centre fold with a damp cloth or steam iron.

If your edge has been woven slightly too tightly at the fold, straighten 2 adjacent threads at the centre and rearrange your threads at regular intervals.

Lampshade

Before starting see:
Finishing Stitch - Mohair Wool

MATERIALS: 1 'American' style lampshade frame, 50 cm in diameter, 1 large darning needle, 1 kitchen fork, 150 g bouclé wool, 50 g mohair wool, 50 g unspun cotton, 100 g warp cotton.

WARP: Stretch your cotton from the bottom circle of the frame to the top one to make the warp.

Make a knot around one of the joins in the bottom circle of the frame and proceed to the top circle. Since this circle is slightly smaller than the lower one, wrap the wool around it 4 times before returning to the lower circle, wrap the wool around the lower one 5 times and return to the top, wrap wool around 4 times and proceed to lower circle, etc.

WEAVING: Proceed as if darning, picking up every other thread with a large darning needle. When you have finished one row beat down the wool with the help of the kitchen fork and weave a second row inverting the stitches, invert again in the third row, weaving it the same as the 1st row, etc.

On the 5th row thread the needle with 2 mohair threads and 2 bouclé threads—turn to 'Finishing Stitch'—and do 1 row of this stitch. To keep the four threads firmly positioned oversew 1 thread in 4 rather than every other thread. This will give a kind of relief stitch. Work another 10 rows in darning stitch in bouclé and on the last row work a normal row of finishing stitch (one and a half times the circumference of the lampshade).

Leave 3 cm unwoven.

Work 1 row in mohair and oversew with finishing stitch, continue with 4 rows darning stitch in this wool and finish with another finishing stitch.

Leave another 3 cm unwoven.

Work 1 more row mohair and oversew with finishing stitch, work 5 more rows and finish with finishing stitch.

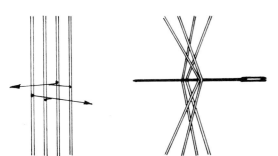

Net Curtaining (1.10 m × 2.60 m)

Form the last band of unwoven threads into Mexican openwork. Thread your needle with a length of mohair wool 1½ times the circumference of the shade.

Join the thread to one of the frame uprights in the centre of the unwoven band. Pass the 2 threads immediately after the join over the 2 following threads. To hold the cross you have made in position, pass the needle between these 4 threads. Pass the 2 following threads over the next 2 and fix into position with the needle, etc. When you come back to the upright tie the two ends of the thread together.

When you have finished the openwork continue weaving, starting 6 cm above the last band. Work a finishing stitch in mohair wool, followed by 1 row. Then thread your needle with unspun cotton and again do the relief finishing stitch. Finish with 1 row mohair and finishing stitch.

Form the unwoven band into double Mexican openwork.

Fix your thread one third of the way up the band and make the first series of openings. When you have gone right round tie the 2 ends of mohair together. Start another set of openings 2 cm above the preceding one. If you tie your thread to a different upright you can alternate your openwork (the threads which went over now are the under threads).

Start again with bouclé wool 1 cm from the previous band and work a row of finishing stitch. Work a 6 cm band in darning stitch. Finish with a row of finishing stitch.

1.5 cm from this last band work an ordinary finishing stitch in mohair.

Leave 4 cm unwoven.

Finish with bouclé, starting with the usual finishing stitch. In the middle of this band work 1 row relief finishing stitch, with your needle threaded with bouclé and unspun cotton.

Before starting see:
Finishing Stitch - Mohair Wool - Finishing

MATERIALS: 300 g mohair, 4 50 g balls cotton, 1 50 g ball pearlised cotton

WARP

Table loom: few alternating reed looms are 1.10 m wide, but you can make this net curtaining as wide as your loom will allow, threading the reed to its maximum width.

The warp is 3 m long. For the distribution of threads follow the instructions given for the four-shaft loom.

Four-shaft loom: Make a warp of 3.20 m, distributing the threads in the following way: 6 mohair threads + 12 cotton threads + 18 mohair threads + 24 cotton + 8 mohair + 16 cotton + 20 mohair + 16 pearlised cotton + 4 mohair + 22 cotton + 4 mohair + 16 pearlised cotton + 8 mohair + 24 cotton + 26 mohair + 16 cotton + 6 mohair = 246 threads.

The alternating bands of different materials and their irregular distribution give the appearance of net curtaining.

The mohair is threaded with 2 dents per cm, the cotton with 4 dents per cm. The pearlised cotton is threaded double with 4 dents per cm.

Leave a space of 8 dents between each of the different materials.

Thread a no. 4 reed using every other dent (or for the table loom thread 1 slot and 1 hole, miss 1 slot and 1 hole, thread 1 slot and 1 hole, etc.) for your 6 mohair threads. Leave 8 dents free, thread your 12 cotton threads through the next 12 dents. Leave 8 dents free, thread the following 18 mohair threads using every other dent. Leave 8 dents free, etc.

For the pearlised cotton thread 2 threads per dent.

The heddles are threaded for serge pattern:

	4	4	4
	3	3	3
	2	2	2
1	1	1	etc.

WEAVING: Stitch used is plain weave, and the weft is entirely in mohair. Start with a row of finishing stitch and work 20 cm. Finish this band with a second row of finishing stitch. Leave 5 cm unwoven warp (to provide horizontal openwork sections). Start another 20 cm band, finished at both ends with a row of finishing stitch. Leave another 5 cm unwoven warp, start a 3rd band of weaving, etc.

Continue in this way until you have worked 9 bands, interspaced with 5 cm unwoven warp, and finish with a 10th band of 30 cm.

Cut off the weaving 10 cm beyond the last finishing stitch, remove from loom and press. Sew curtain tape along the top and reinforce the bottom with extra rows of stitching, or leave small fringes.